no matter what

A STORY OF
A CHILD PRODIGY

RUTH TOPACIO REYES

ISBN: 978-1-965341-11-7
eBook also available

FIRST EDITION

TWO PENNY
PUBLISHING

Two Penny Publishing is a partnership publisher of a variety of genres. We help first-time and seasoned authors share their stories, passion, knowledge, and experiences that help others grow and learn. Please visit our website, TwoPennyPublishing.com if you would like us to consider your manuscript or book idea for publishing.

To Elizur, Miriam, and Melissa

"I found my home in our family."

Ruth Topacio Reyes tells stories like a great home cook who makes a meal without much fuss but with depth and flair. Her memorable experiences fill us with satisfaction. The tales she relates resonate with the details she lovingly provides and the big-picture lessons we can all benefit from. It is a powerful reminder of the individuality of struggle and the common threads of our shared humanity. The confluence of stories about the Philippines, New York, Beethoven, the Beatles, Juilliard, and Queens College is a heartfelt whirlwind.

—**EDWARD SMALDONE, Ph.D.**
Professor Emeritus, Aaron Copland School of Music, Composer, most recent CD: *What no one else sees...* (New Focus Recordings, 2024), New York City

Ruth Reyes is an extremely talented pianist, but the message of this book extends far beyond the field of music. Anyone who wants to make the most of their God-given talent in any field can benefit from the principles of mental and physical discipline advocated in these pages. To make the most of what God has given you should be everyone's goal because, as Ruth writes, "A talent is a gift that must be shared for the greater good." Read this inspirational book and discover how a person can be extremely gifted without becoming the stereotypical eccentric artist.

—**BOB RUSSELL**
Retired Senior Minister, Southeast Christian Church, Author of *When God Builds a Church* and *After 50 Years of Ministry: 7 Things I'd Do Differently and 7 Things I'd Do the Same*, Louisville, Kentucky

No Matter What: A Story of a Child Prodigy is a moving journey through the highs and lows of extraordinary talent. Ruth Topacio Reyes masterfully captures the struggles and triumphs of a gifted child navigating the complexities of life as an artist, an immigrant, a woman of color, and a person of deep faith. Reyes offers readers a tale of resilience, determination, and the power of discipline—artistic and spiritual. Ruth invites readers to reflect on their own "Carnegie Hall," their highest aspirations. *No Matter What* is a must-read for artists searching for guidance in navigating the high-pressure world of world-class performance and readers seeking a heartfelt story of the beauty in perseverance and the strength of unconditional love. Reyes's storytelling is as captivating as it is uplifting—an absolute gem.

—GARY DAVID STRATTON, Ph.D.
Dean of the School of Arts and Sciences, Johnson University, Author of *The Jesus Climb: Journeying from Student to Disciple*, Knoxville, Tennessee

Dr. Reyes, a true child prodigy, vividly recounts her journey in a way that transports readers into her world. Every detail comes alive, from the tender moments of practicing and traveling with her mother to lessons and performances to the courage to leave her family in the Philippines to attend Juilliard. You feel her loneliness, heartache, and relentless determination as she navigates the hall of one of the world's most prestigious institutions. Her story is a testament to resilience and passion, inspiring readers to pursue their dreams and unwavering dedication, no matter the sacrifices.

—BRENDA JACKSON, M.Ed.
Retired Administrator, Central Islip School District, Long Island, New York

Ruth Topacio Reyes shares an engaging, entertaining, and inspiring reflection on her rich musical life. Filled with great insights into the importance and value of discipline and dedication to her lifelong artistic pursuits, it is presented in a natural and winsome style that feels like a visit with a close—and extremely talented—friend.

—CHRISTOPHER CONFESSORE
Music Director, Brevard Symphony Orchestra,
Principal POPS Conductor,
Alabama Symphony Orchestra

Dr. Reyes has drawn upon her unique and inspiring life story to explore essential principles for developing a godly character and a productive career. She communicates a positive, healthy definition of a disciplined life, identifies the good habits necessary for this discipline, and models the kind of gritty perseverance that allows one to finish well. These are lessons that benefit anyone from all walks of life—child prodigy or not!

—L. THOMAS (TOMMY) SMITH, JR., Ph.D.
President Emeritus, Johnson University, Author of
*Above Every Other Desire: A History of Johnson University,
1893-2018*, Knoxville, Tennessee

Ruth Reyes embodies the unique blend of challenge and privilege that comes with being labeled a child prodigy. Her extraordinary musical talent shines brightly, but her exceptional leadership truly sets her apart. With profound wisdom and rich experiences, she has inspired countless young people and leaders alike. Ruth invites us to accompany her on a journey through her childhood and career, uncovering timeless principles that anyone can adopt to realize their full potential. As the saying goes, "The artist is nothing without the gift, and the gift is nothing without the work." Dive into Ruth's book and discover the transformative lessons of harnessing a gift to create something truly extraordinary.

—**RICK RUSAW**
Executive Director, Spire Network, Executive Team, Gloo, Author of *The Externally Focused Church*, *Living a Life on Loan* and *The Externally Focused Quest*

Ruth Topacio Reyes delicately orchestrated the book, weaving lessons on discipline with personal anecdotes. Playing for royalty as a child leading to being a teenage immigrant, learning to navigate the subway system from Queens to Juilliard (while bouncing a tuning fork on her leg), she is equipped to teach us all a bit more about healthy habits as a foundation for a life that cultivates any God-given giftings. As a digital artist, I learned from Ruth how she balanced her creativity strengths with discipline, faith with nose-to-the-grind work ethic, confidence with humility, and always bringing honor to the Giver of Gifts.

—**CRYSTAL HUTCHESON**
Senior Graphic Designer, Action Church, Orlando, Florida

There are very few child prodigies in the world. We hear or see them on television and we're amazed and awed. Observers of their brilliance might think to themselves, "I wish I could play like that." Perhaps after reading the book, you might recant that wish! The book captures the intense nature of the process behind the development of a child possessing extraordinary talent. The life story is told with incredible and uncanny detail with insights about what it truly takes to become great. You will cheer on the author as she shares her unique adventures with music, culture, faith, and family. I highly recommend this book and "no matter what, don't stop; take it to the end."

—SUSAN TORBENSON, Ed.D.
Educator, Dissertation Chair, Nova Southeastern University, Green Bay, Wisconsin

God blessed Dr. Ruth Reyes with extraordinary musical talent. Committed to stewarding this gift faithfully, she intentionally and tenaciously developed her abilities and used them to honor God, bless His people, and mentor countless more. Her testimony inspires, challenges, and encourages. You will be blessed by reading her story and insights.

—DANIEL OVERDORF, M.Div., D.Min.
President, Johnson University, Author of *Preaching: A Simple Approach to the Sacred Task*, Knoxville, Tennessee

Starting as a sheltered prodigy in the Philippines, Ruth shares her fascinating and uplifting journey of discovering her independent musician self and identity as a citizen of God's kingdom. Her story testifies to how talent, teachers, sacrifice, hard work, and the driving forces of family and determination converge to cultivate a music career—which can look profoundly different decades later.

—ESTHER CHUNG MARKS
Pianist and Teacher, President, Suffolk Music Teachers Foundation, Port Jefferson Station, New York

From her hardworking childhood in Manila to Juilliard to the present day, Ruth's story helps us understand what it means to be successful, not only as a musician but as a human. Her unique and fascinating memoir is full of wisdom and practical insights. I'm so grateful for her example!

—JENNIFER JOHNSON
Director of Research Marketing, University of Tennessee, Author of *See Jen Write*, Knoxville, Tennessee

Dr. Ruth Reyes has given us a colorful memoir about music, performance, family, discipline, influence, and godliness. It reads just as anyone who has heard her playing or conversation would expect: clear, focused, illuminating. Thanks, Ruth, for taking it to the end!

—JON WEATHERLY, Ph.D.
Associate Pastor, Twin City Bible Church, Formerly Provost and Professor of New Testament, Johnson University, Author of *1 & 2 Thessalonians* (College Press NIV Commentary), Urbana, Illinois

No Matter What is a delightful peek into an extraordinary life. From Manila to New York City, from child prodigy to child-rearing, Ruth has filled the pages of her book with memories of fascinating encounters, formative mentors, and a myriad of lessons learned along the way. Her book is a testament to the value of each of our unique lives and a challenge to live every moment with purpose and intention.

—BILL WOLF, D.W.S., O.S.L.
Professor of Worship & Theology, Director of Worship Leadership Program, Johnson University, Songwriter, most recent musical project: "52 Songs in 52 Weeks" (billwolfmusic.com, 2024), Knoxville, Tennessee

As you join Dr. Reyes on a journey through her incredible (at times unbelievable) life experiences you can't help being taken in by her authenticity and vulnerability. You don't have to be a child prodigy or a concert pianist to benefit from the wisdom and sensible, practical application she gained along the way. Her never-stop-learning approach to life is simply inspiring. *No Matter What: A Story of a Child Prodigy* challenges you to resolve to "not stop and take it to the end."

—MARK MONTEMAYOR
Executive Coach, Founder of Leadership Clarity, Clermont, Florida

In sharing her remarkable journey, Dr. Ruth Reyes invites readers on an expedition of self-discovery. Ruth's personal stories allow readers to reflect on developing their own talents as they discover that the road doesn't always go where they might expect. Ruth proves that life is, indeed, a journey that should be filled with purpose and meaning. May we all live so well.

—MATTHEW BROADDUS, Ph.D.

Associate Provost for Accreditation, Dean of the School of Communication and Creative Arts, Johnson University, Author of *Phineas Bleak and the Shadows of Elkmont* and *Phineas Bleak and the Ghost of the Past*, Knoxville, Tennessee

Told through the lens of a unique life journey filled with challenges, hard work, amazing blessings, a strong family, exceptional teachers, and God's guiding hand, *No Matter What* offers an inspiring and engaging invitation to discipline and intentionality. Anyone desiring to steward their God-given gifts and talents for maximum impact should take this journey.

—BRIAN D. SMITH, Ph.D.

President, Dallas Christian College, Dallas, Texas

From her fascinating Filipino household to city streets, practice rooms and concert halls, Ruth Reyes will draw you into her unique story. While especially inspirational for pianists, her captivating narrative is enriched by lessons learned and advice for anyone seeking to embrace discipline in their own life. Written with candor, humor, and self-reflection, *No Matter What* will keep you intrigued and leave you motivated to reflect upon your own path.

—DINELLE FRANKLAND, D.W.S.

Professor, The Robert E. Webber Institute for Worship Studies, Author of *His Story, Our Response: What the Bible Says About Worship*, Jacksonville, Florida

The book is the telling of a Filipino music prodigy's disciplined life. Ruth's talent, her hard work, the education she received, coupled with the support and the safe environment her family provided, all propelled her to develop her musical ability, and more. She thrived in the environment of Juilliard, but read also about her journey to self-discovery, beyond the singular identity of concert pianist.

—KENTARO YAMAMOTO, Ph.D.
Deputy Director, Center for Global Assessment,
Educational Testing Service, Princeton, New Jersey

No Matter What is a captivating story of perseverance, resilience, and unshakable faith. Ruth Topacio Reyes creates a very enjoyable journey for the reader. Packed with invaluable life lessons, her story not only deeply inspired me, but will also uplift your spirit and encourage you to pursue your dreams with unwavering determination.

—SCOTT EYNON
Pastor, Community Christian Church,
Ft. Lauderdale, Florida

The book offers a glimpse into the author's life growing up as a child prodigy and the lessons learned. Ruth provides valuable insights into the discipline required to become an outstanding performer, sharing anecdotes from her experiences to illustrate the points. The narrative is intricately woven into a life story that is still unfolding.

—JOHN T. SARNO
Worship Consultant, Resource Pastor in Worship Arts,
Worship Ministry Enrichment, Bel Air, Maryland

I love the book. It's practical and inspirational. You write very well, Ruth. I am honored to have been a small part of your God story. You are a gift to the church. We need female voices like yours who speak into conservative Christianity. I am so proud of your good work and how God used you.

—TOM JONES, M.Div., D.Min.
Church Planter, Author of *Church Planting from the Ground Up*, Lakeside, Ohio

The book is an inspiring journey of a talented musician and teacher. Ruth highlights her transition from Manila to Juilliard, focusing on the significance of discipline and good practice habits. As her former student, I've felt her profound impact on my musical development. She embodies the idea that "to teach is to touch a life forever." Her encouragement in the words "no matter what" inspires me to be the teacher I am today.

—LAURIE BROOKS, D.W.S.
Professor, School of Music, Liberty University, Lynchburg, Virginia

CONTENTS

FOREWORD

A quick search on Google reveals a "prodigy" is "a person, especially a young one, endowed with exceptional qualities or abilities."

Dr. Ruth Reyes is the only prodigy I've ever known, and per the definition above, she is absolutely endowed with exceptional qualities like:

Wisdom
Grace
Compassion
Kindness
Intelligence
Grit
Character

Oh, and she can play the piano—and write—pretty well, too!

This book, like Ruth, is a treasure…it's exceptional! I was captivated from the first word until the last.

This book, *No Matter What: A Story of a Child Prodigy*, by Dr. Ruth Topacio Reyes chronicles her journey as a talented pianist, navigating life's challenges and triumphs with resilience, discipline, and faith. Structured around her experiences from childhood in the Philippines to becoming a concert pianist, the memoir blends personal anecdotes with reflections on perseverance, the importance of good habits, and the transformative power of music.

I believe this book will endow you with valuable knowledge, wisdom, perspective, and inspiration. I believe I'm a better human for reading this book.

Why? Lots of reasons, but here are five:

First, this book teaches the importance of discipline and tenacity: Ruth describes how her early exposure to rigorous practice routines and discipline shaped her character and artistry. She details how growing up in a traditional Filipino household with high expectations, led her to develop a strong work ethic that supported her musical career.

Second, this book details the importance of cultural and familial influences: Ruth describes how her Filipino heritage, family dynamics, and the guidance of her maternal grandfather, "Daddy," deeply impacted her outlook on life and music.

Third, this book inspires with lessons on faith and purpose: Throughout the book, Ruth emphasizes her gratitude to God for her talents and her commitment to using them purposefully. She draws parallels between her journey and biblical lessons on stewardship.

Fourth, this book explains the power of music as a universal language: From her early days at the piano to performing on renowned stages, Ruth highlights how music connected her to audiences and her family, especially her father.

Fifth, this book is a blessing because my friend, Ruth, believes that you—as made in the image of God—have also been endowed with exceptional qualities and abilities, too.

—**Arron Chambers**, Pastor, Consultant,
and Author of eight books, including
Love Better and *Eats with Sinners*

PREFACE

"No matter what happens, you don't stop. You take it to the end!"

I vividly remembered these words, pronounced in an encouraging, mellow tone, paired with a punctuated gravity in his voice. My piano teacher, the late Leon Pommers, was a source of inspiration. His words guided me through many solo recitals and ensemble concerts, but for some reason, I heard them again, swiftly crashing through my distracted circumstance like the force of a rushing river. I sat on a stage in front of the grand piano in the middle of a performance in Knoxville, Tennessee, and listened.

I was invited to perform a 30-minute Monday night concert set at a summer conference at Johnson University (JU). It wasn't the typical college audience, as it was the university's Renew conference. The university hosts three identical weeks of Renew. Each week provides on-site housing and dining and a mixed bag of spiritual development, field trips, and entertainment programming for people over fifty.

It was the third week. I was performing the Chopin Revolutionary Etude, a piece I had already played the two previous Mondays. In the middle of the piece, Mr. Pommers' mantra flashed through my mind out of nowhere—"No matter what happens, you don't stop. You take it to the end!" It was during a most inopportune time. With the third performance, I figured I would be in and out—easy-peasy—so I thought.

The performance was flawless until, at one minute and seventeen seconds into the two-minute and forty-seven-second piece, there was complete darkness. At first, I thought it was either one of those rare cases of being struck blind for no apparent reason or, more likely, a power surge. It turned out that both options were wishful thinking.

I found out after the program that the entire side of the mountain that runs the length of JU's campus was entirely in the dark. There was a major power malfunction leading to a brownout. Well, how does one deal with a power glitch in the middle of a series of Chopin speeding sixteenth notes? I practiced in the dark many times when I was a child growing up in the Philippines. Thanks to monsoons knocking out the power, I had many opportunities to hone my like-blindfolded playing skills. No big deal!

The night of the brownout, I kept on playing. I did not stop, though I found myself slightly slowing down the tempo of the etude. I'm sure it was a startled, knee-jerk reaction from being plunged into the dark. Then, within a second or two, I heard my teacher's bidding, "No matter what . . . take it to the end." I had been trained to do precisely that. It should be my default response to the call. So, in the dark, I kept playing, committed to taking Chopin to its conclusion.

There was no stopping the flurry of notes cascading down the ivory keys to the very last four chords. I was beyond determined to complete the performance, no matter what. And then a miracle happened! Well, sort of. The technical director came to my rescue with another 50-60 seconds remaining. He flashed a tiny beam of flashlight from the back of the auditorium to shine just enough light on the piano keys to guide me to the end.

I have thought a lot about that night since then. I began writing during a more than-normally-packed academic year. My personal goal was to complete the writing within two years. The first 50 pages of the book came easily. The writing was fast and furious. I recall thinking how the Baroque composer Handel, in composing *The Messiah* in 23 days, must have experienced a similar but an even more acute kind of frenzied behavior—a divine inspiration perhaps. Details of childhood memories, life-changing events, and defining moments swept in with clarity and speed. I was amazed at how the creative aptitude appeared to come from nowhere. I was convinced there was no delaying the urgency to tell my story.

Maneuvering through the stream of distractions, both personal and professional, I faced a challenge that became more pronounced each day, and suddenly, my goal to finish the book became insurmountable. Relationships needed attention. Work-related projects began to pile up. Rest and relaxation became scarce or more tiring than it should be. Health issues increased. Doctor's visits, tests, and more tests consumed my time. I didn't see any other option but the obvious and right decision to put the project on hold. An opportunity to resume writing came in the summer of 2018 with newer insights, with more focus, and an appreciation of God's timing. The reason for the respite from writing became crystallized within a few days. There was to be a period of silence for more discovery and reflection. I began to understand what exactly carried me and what continues to carry me through life's journey.

I have been blessed with a talent. To have been dubbed a child music prodigy is something I did not seek. I remember the first time I heard it or read about it, as a matter of fact. My picture during the performance, attached to a short article, was in the arts and entertainment section of the local newspaper. There I was, a piano soloist with the orchestra, a little girl in her frilly concert attire. I knew as a young child that my life was different from my siblings and my peers. It was equal parts real and surreal. It was like a child's play, but I lived it in an adult world, within societal expectations. That was my life, and it wasn't easy. This book is a compilation of my journal entries about that kind of life, at times enchanting but without the glamor, pretension, and glare of today's popular reality TV fare. It is about good habits that foundationally grounded my life, as seen through the lens of a wide-eyed young immigrant from the other side of the world, navigating the demands of a new American culture and its expectations while pursuing the technical and artistic development of a blossoming musical career. It is about tenacity and living life with no regrets.

The purpose of the book is to inspire any person to achieve a goal with intentionality. Oftentimes, we trudge through life without a plan or embrace the *que sera sera* attitude, in English, "whatever will be will be." But life is a gift, a gift that must be stewarded and tended. Though not a how-to book, I provide suggestions and tips on how to take the first steps in the practice of discipline and establishing good habits. Life is difficult. The stories of my younger life hopefully will provide the readers with examples of how good habits support sustainability in facing the ongoing demands and obstacles in life. No matter what the challenge may be, take it to the end.

Johann Sebastian Bach, the other noted Baroque composer, was also a church music director in a Lutheran congregation. I have always been an avid consumer of Bach's keyboard repertoire. The depth of his compositional acuity and musicality was equally matched by his dedication to God. Three words of Bach inspire me greatly. His signature on each of his musical compositions constituted a tribute to the Giver of Talents, *Soli Deo Gloria*, abbreviated S.D.G., Latin for "Glory to God alone." I write to call attention to the fact that who God is and what He has done for us calls us to give Him glory. I write to attest to God's generosity and faithfulness in my life. The late Eugene Peterson put it this way, from Psalm 9:1, "I'm thanking you, God, from a full heart. I'm writing [a] book on your wonders."

1 | A MATTER OF DISCIPLINE

My musical life started in the Philippines when I was five years old. Filipino kids usually call their fathers *Tatay* and their mothers *Nanay*. My family gravitated more to calling our father Papa and our mother Mama, a residual of the 300-year Spanish rule and influence on our island nation. The Tagalog word for grandfather is *Lolo*, and for grandmother, *Lola*. But my maternal grandfather, the patriarch of the extended family, insisted that his grandchildren call him Daddy. A few other names of uncles, aunts, sisters, and brothers will appear as we go along.

American business-es began to emerge in Manila after World War II. Daddy was

> Discipline is to submit to the promise of getting better and better at one thing through laborious repetitions.

employed as a bookkeeper at a local Ford Motors office in Manila. Daddy's hospitable nature brought family, friends, neighbors, church family, and coworkers to his house, where I got to meet his American friends. No one in our large extended family had ever been called Daddy before, and I wondered why he wanted to be called that. But Daddy had American friends and coworkers, and I am only guessing now that he wanted to be called Daddy, the English word for father, because of an affinity with the Americans.

My Papa and Mama, two younger sisters, and later a baby brother, and I lived in Daddy's big house. Eventually, uncles, aunts, and cousins lived in smaller houses or dormers annexed to the big house, all in the same compound. Such was life in Manila, as I remember it. Stories of my formative years and reflections as an adult will flow in and out of the narrative.

My point of view was shaped by, first and foremost, my Filipino family, crazy, comfortable but not rich by Filipino standards, goal-oriented yet dysfunctional, loving, but with super high expectations; secondly, the intersection of my God-given talents and my basic temperament; lastly, the sum of my experiences, both good and bad. I hope that there is something here for any reader to rediscover the truth, take away a lesson or two, and find inspiration to take a similar "no matter what" kind of journey.

It took me years to realize that a "no matter what" kind of statement is a matter of discipline. Growing up, I viewed the word discipline with guarded trepidation. I attended an all-girl K-12 Catholic school in Manila. Nuns ruled! Enough said. Sister Principal had rules and regulations for everything. The skirt hem of our immaculately starched and ironed uniforms could not be shorter than just above the knees. Any slight deviation in hem length and you, and other similar offenders, would be called up in front of the general assembly to suffer through a painstaking ritual of passing or failing the tape measurement test. I managed to avoid embarrassment by being a compliant student. I followed the rules—all the rules. Students assembled in a straight line with heads aligned in a row like military cadets. When the bell rang, we filed quietly and walked like tiptoeing soldiers, never out of line, almost in unison, and almost not breathing, if at all possible. Never mind the fact that we were carrying, dragging is probably a better word, 10-12 textbooks and 10-12 notebooks in our hand-carried school bag at a time when backpacks were not in vogue.

Silence was to be observed at all times when you walked down the hallways. Classroom rules of conduct were even more exhaustive and prescriptive: How to address teachers and authorities; how to answer a question; how to raise your hand to answer or ask a question; where and how to stand within your row of student desks; how to pass a paper from back to front; how to be excused to leave the classroom; how to sit properly; how to show respect for one another. So many rules! Being sent to the principal's office signaled that you were in trouble for breaking one of the rules. The measure of your punishment and the kind of discipline meted out depended on the gravity of the rule-breaking, or simply, the gravity of your sin. I say sin because, in a Catholic environment, it was more than possible that a particular broken rule might necessitate a trip to the confessional, needing an absolution. That made me doubly scared of discipline.

Discipline anchors the talent. At home, discipline was preceded by a moment of silence, almost like a religious experience in full view of the extended family. Brothers, sisters, cousins, second cousins, aunts, uncles, grandmothers, my mother and father, and other relatives who I thought were relatives but who were not, all lined up as though to witness an execution. And the executioner was someone who demanded the solemnity of the occasion and who relished all the "uh-ohs" and "oh nos" buzzing through his courtroom. The judge was Daddy, a self-made man, an utmost disciplinarian! There was no reasoning or bargaining with him. You were judged guilty when one of his rules was disobeyed. No such thing as due process. What did we expect, a democracy? The word *discipline* rightfully evoked the fear of God among us, but even more so, the fear of Daddy's wrath. But then again, none of us in my generation ever thought that we were living under an authoritarian kind of rule. It was just the norm for the family.

According to the English Oxford Dictionary, the first definition of discipline is *the practice of training people to obey rules or a code of behavior, using punishment to correct disobedience.*[1] The kind of discipline dished out by Sister Principal and Daddy. But let's consider another definition of discipline: *An activity or experience that provides mental or physical training. Or when used as a verb it means to train oneself to do something in a controlled and habitual way.*[2] This is the kind of discipline that is intentional and not reactionary. It is cultivated over time, bears good fruit, and is sustainable. It is rooted in commitment and hard work. Discipline is to submit to the promise of getting better and better at one thing through laborious repetitions. It is goal-oriented with measurable good outcomes—that no matter what, you persevere through the obstacles and challenges to take whatever it is you are tackling to the end.

This pursuit of discipline that bears good fruit is demonstrated no better than in the arenas of sports and music, where live action or live performance is played out on center stage. Athletes and artists are performers, each in their own way. They produce something for an audience that may be competitive, entertaining, and

> Discipline is rooted in something as simple as basic good habits.

inspiring, all at the same time. Athletes and artists devote hours to exercise and preparation, a rigor that demands total commitment to the goal. The tedious road to a single performance could entail a laborious process of blood, sweat, and tears. Artists and athletes subscribe to this kind of pain because they can visualize the expected outcomes. They submit to the diligence of practice and instinctively know that the plethora of sacrifices that accompany this kind of pursuit will be worth it in the end.

In *Mastering the Art of Performance*, Stewart Gordon reminds the artist that in "preparing for your performance, remember that virtually every performer comes to the point of having to use plain old-fashioned discipline to keep the process going."[3] There are no ifs and buts; if you want to perform well, you must do the time. So, how do you cultivate discipline to develop your talent? What does the stewardship of a talent look like? A popular quote on talent is from

Establishing good habits early in life is the foundation for developing a disciplined life.

author Leo Buscaglia, "Your talent is God's gift to you; what you do with it is your gift to God."[4]

I believe that being talented is not enough. Talent starts as a raw ingredient, and it begs to be cultivated into the promise of a fine product. It is a gift. It begins as a potential, but what you do with what you have been given is up to you. Many external factors can affect its development or non-development, or whether it will be used for good or bad. The potential must be complemented by hard work and good progress over time. It takes time to see the final product. But if what you do with the talent determines the acceptable or unacceptable outcome, how does one set out to protect the talent, be responsible for it, and achieve the desired outcome?

The accounting of talents in Matthew 25:14-30 is a good example of the final analysis of measuring our talents. In the parable of the talents, each of the three people was given a different amount or number of talents depending on their ability. Each person was charged to do their best with their given talent. While two of them invested and used their talents to successfully double what they had been given, one buried the talent and gained nothing more. At the end of my life, I would like to think that I would be able to have a conversation with Jesus and tell Him the stories of my transformed life because of His crazy love for me. Likewise, at the end of my life, I will be held responsible for and must give an account of what I did with what I have been gifted. It's an accountability issue. I probably should pause, ponder, and prepare to answer the Giver of Talents whether I've been faithful with the talents placed in my trust. The question is, how does one grow the talents?

Discipline anchors the talent. It is what helps grow the talent. But discipline is not a fluky happenstance; it presupposes a plan. Discipline subscribes to a prescriptive set of procedures, and there has to be a commitment to the plan. Discipline, in cultivating talent, becomes a way of life so that the talent can grow and bear good fruit in a healthy environment over time. Subscribing to a values-driven lifestyle of diligence, commitment to the long haul, and determination to complete a task is daunting, but in the end will be most rewarding. But if discipline anchors the talent, how does discipline become a way of life? What is its solid foundation?

A talent is a gift that must be shared for the greater good.

From my own experience, I will say that discipline is rooted in something as simple as basic good habits, which are formed early on in a person's development. Tom Paterson in *The Life You Were Meant to Live* calls it the winter of early youth, when "you internalize the framework that you will carry with you all your life."[5] Brushing your teeth two times a day, doing your homework, going to bed early, making your bed, doing your chores regularly, being punctual, being polite, eating healthily, and exercising daily are a few examples of basic good habits. Seymour Fink adds, "The pianist practices to acquire the habits that will create the musical meanings he or she seeks."[6] Developing good habits is elemental to setting up the steady rhythms of life. More than just routines that may pass by in meaningless strides, good habits are firmly grounded and purposeful. Good habits build discipline and character.

Keeping up with good habits has significant implications on other aspects of life that may carry through to your adult life. Good or bad habits stay with you for a long time and filter down through the different phases of your life. So, choosing wisely early could benefit you in the long run. Practicing good habits also presupposes a repetitive action. It demands self-control and tenacity to stay with the program, or you can easily fall out of habit. It begins with a reasonable schedule you can handle, which you can later adjust as the discipline becomes a way of life. Establishing good habits early in life is the foundation for developing a disciplined life; the younger you get started, the better, for it is just as easy to cultivate bad habits. It does not take much for it to happen. Matthew 26:41 has been used as an idiom to denote weakness: "The spirit is willing, but the flesh is weak."[7] So either you will have a solid foundation or a poor foundation.

When the opportunity to learn a new skill is presented, as in sports or music, the disciplined routine it calls for will become familiar as each day, each week, or each month passes by because you will have become accustomed to habitual practice and repetition. One example of this is getting up early in the morning to walk three miles. During the first few days or maybe even an entire week, getting out of bed each morning will be the most difficult to conquer. You will try to find every excuse you can muster not to stand up, get ready, and go out the door. Let the repetition and resolve to make it an everyday event win over the excuses. It's the day-in, day-out practice of good habits that prepare you for harder work later on, or as the Bible puts it in Luke 16:10, "Whoever can be trusted with very little can also be trusted with much."[8]

When I asked Mama if I could take piano lessons as soon as I turned five, I remember her asking me several times if I was sure it was what I wanted. She insisted that taking lessons shouldn't be on a whim; that once I began, it would mean setting up a scheduled time for practice every day. Though I did not fully comprehend at the time what the impact of practicing would be on my very young life, I agreed to the deal. I did not recall signing any contract, but Mama knew what the drill was going to be like for her eldest child, for she was a former music major. Practicing shortly commenced after the first lesson, albeit we were only at the beginning level of piano playing: the regular finger strengthening through a group of finger exercises, the learning of new music, and the reviewing and memorizing of all recently learned music. It was a breeze, I thought. The practice routine settled down comfortably, a familiar rhythmic pattern in my daily life. Mama saw to it that good practice habits were established early on. It's these habits I learned as a child that would set me up for the rigor of what was about to come.

Chasing fame and glory becomes a personal goal for many, whether it's of one's choosing or the imposition by well-meaning folks and loved ones who believed a talent should not go to waste and who were convinced that talent, if developed, nurtured, and demonstrated, could almost always provide the ticket to a better life. Becoming so dedicated to the craft that a few might call it a "calling" is an upstanding and noble commitment. This is true whether you have the talent of an artist or an athlete. The pathway is prescriptive. Artists and athletes dedicate long hours of practice every day to prepare to get that one shot of a stellar performance. They develop work ethics that become second nature to them. Work hard to achieve your target, give 100%, and execute as close to perfection as possible. Build a level of endurance so you can tackle the difficult components of the training and sustain your level of concentration during the performance. Be flexible and confident to make quick decisions to adjust for any misstep or unavoidable challenge in performance. Embrace the opportunity to inspire.

A talent is a gift that must be shared for the greater good.

2 | HOW DO YOU GET TO CARNEGIE HALL?

The question, with the accompanying punchline, is called "The Carnegie Joke." It has been credited as being one of the famous one-liners of the late celebrity comedian Jack Benny. It has also been ascribed to virtuoso musicians like the late pianist great Arthur Rubenstein, who truly understood the hard road to the iconic venue. Yet still, several folks believe that the joke and punchline could also have come from a nameless street musician, one of hundreds that you might meet at various corners or on subway platforms of New York City. No one knows its origin for certain. A recital at Carnegie Hall in New York City is the epitome of success, the dream final destination of an accomplished world-class musician. Carnegie Hall is one of the most prestigious and venerable institutions for classical and popular music. However, my Uncle Mel did not hold a natural liking to anything that even faintly resembled Carnegie Hall music material, maybe Carnegie Hall architecture and stage design, for he was an architect by trade. But he was a huge fan of Frank Sinatra. Having lived in New York since the late 1960s, his favorite song was the Ol' Blue Eyes' hit "New York, New York," ranked third among Sinatra's greatest hits. "My Way" comes in first, and "Fly Me to the Moon" second. Uncle Mel, in a not-so-subtle tone, but in his best attempt to encourage, would remind me time and time again in the words of his idol, "If you can make it there, [in New York], you'll make it anywhere."

A performance within Carnegie's hallowed walls and halls trumpets, "You made it to the top!" But imagine just for a second the joke's implication that a nitty-gritty arduous journey of countless hours of practice and preparation is what it takes to get to that place. It means choosing a less-traveled road that only the resilient may be equipped or, at best, willing to take. Practice, to a musician, may mean at least two to three hours a day. Practice, practice, is double the hours. Practice! Practice! Practice! Well, that's practically your entire day.

Thomas Sterner proposes in *The Practicing Mind* that "learning to walk and to articulate our thoughts and feelings started from a place of no skill" and that "we acquired these skills by the process we call practice."[1] He adds, "all of life is practice, in one form or another" and gives a personal anecdote that he "mistakenly associated the word practice only with art forms such as music, dance, and painting."[2] Embracing the fullness of the truth of how practice impacts not only the acquisition of specific skills but also how it has lifelong implications in character formation was a far cry from a child prodigy's limited grasp of discipline, that was only measured by how many taxing hours she had to spend to get to a place of being performance-ready. The real benefits of a disciplined life are not easily deduced or appreciated at a young age. One can even surmise that the burden of repetitive routine and the kind of blinders-on focus might limit a prodigy's long-term vision.

In *The Paradox of Generosity*, Smith and Davidson highlight practices of generosity that not only develop character but also promote happiness, bodily health, and the purpose of living. They describe this tension in habitual actions: "What matters about practices, compared to one-time acts, is that they are repeated behaviors that involve recurrent intention and attention."[3] Repetition is part of the process of developing and fine-tuning any skill which contributes to a better life. Paterson also points out the truth that "We are challenged by God to hone our gifts to the sharpest edge possible . . . to develop mastery of our gifts . . . rooted in practice and more practice and still more practice."[4] The Apostle Paul in 2 Corinthians 9:6 frames this concept in terms of outcomes, "Whoever sows sparingly will also reap sparingly, and whoever sows generously will also reap generously."[5] You reap what you sow.

The regimented life started early for me. Juggling family time, school, church, and music lessons dominated my weeks. I learned what delayed gratification meant before I came across the term in a high school Psychology class. But for all the sacrifices that accompanied this kind of choosing, it also ushered in awards, rewards, and lots of glory. It was what I knew as normal. Practicing during my first three years of piano study lasted two-and-a-half hours a day. It was understandable that at such a young age, I would be oblivious to what was about to invade my life. I had no clue at all what practicing would require. I managed to plow through the "ignorance is bliss" phase that was my early years without much angst. I attended elementary school. I took lessons. I practiced, played recitals, and entered talent competitions. It was a breeze. Life was fun.

Then, when I turned ten, I began conservatory on Saturdays and extended piano lessons on weekdays. It changed everything! The practice demands of conservatory study increased exponentially. The piano solo pieces had reached the advanced level of Baroque, Classical, and Romantic music with a smattering of emerging 20th-century modern music. The list of piano concertos to study also grew. From Mozart to Grieg, each multi-movement work differed in style and musical interpretation. Developing technical precision became a priority. It all translated into long hours of painstakingly meticulous execution of strengthening finger exercises. Preparing for each piano lesson required longer hours. It doubled or tripled the effort altogether. There was no more glossing over musical passages or relying on my fingers to go where they were supposed to go. I had to critically think about each phrasing, each scale run, each theme, and each cadence.

In addition to piano lessons, theory classes meant more written homework and practice. The theory keyboard assignments were something new. I thought I knew a lot about music because I had been playing since I was five, but theory took me by surprise. It's as though I stepped into a fantastical world of hypotheses and new vocabulary with readily available pixie dust to keep me happy and inquisitive for a long time. I never thought I would grow to appreciate it or, as a matter of fact, even love it the more I delved into it. It did not take me long to realize I was a music geek, much more than I'd like to admit. The study of music theory was similar to learning a foreign language and math at the same time. I became intrigued by forms, intervallic relationships, harmony, polyphony, and voice-leading. I began to think that I had a knack for this discovery.

However, musical theory was not confined to writing four parts of harmony on paper. It was also theory in practice. In addition to the written homework, there were chord progressions to practice on the piano. I thought I was through with practicing repetitive technical exercises after having learned every scale and arpeggio on the Circle of Fifths chart. However, the more I advanced into the theory study, the longer the keyboard exercises of chord progressions became, with expectations to transpose the exercises into different keys. Hence, my practice ritual multiplied in intensity and time commitment. Still, I did not complain about the tedious hours. I was hungry to learn more and to produce something creative. I was having fun in the process and that was all that mattered.

Paterson surprisingly wrote specifically about practicing, the seemingly baneful cross musicians carry. His description is on point, "People who are gifted in music generally do not need to be told that they are musically talented. They readily can tell that they have the ability to sing or play a musical instrument. Furthermore, you don't have to tell gifted musicians to enjoy music. They do so automatically. You don't have to browbeat them to practice; they delight in practicing because they enjoy good music and want to be able to play musical pieces to the best of their ability. Gifted musicians never feel better or have a greater sense of purpose and fulfillment than when they are engaged in the performance of their gift. This same combination of excellence, enjoyment, and giftedness exists for every type of talent or combination of talents."[6] Practicing, in essence, is an integral part of the journey for both the artist and the listener. The artist honed their skills, while the listener is poised to appreciate a well-rehearsed performance.

This kind of practice is also specific. Gerald Klickstein, in *The Musician's Way*, emphasizes that "talent symbolizes your underlying potential; practice enables you to realize that potential. But not just any sort of practice will do."[7] Good practice should be focused, deliberate, meticulous, and evaluative. Good practice can reveal repeated mistakes and correct them systematically. That is sometimes how the longer hours should be used to reach the close-to-perfection performance that audiences with discriminating ears will find pleasurable. As the Polish pianist Ignacy Jan Paderewski noted, "If I miss a day of practice, I know it; two days, the critics know it; three days, the audience knows it."[8]

I agree with Sterner when he wrote, "Habits and practice are very interrelated. What we practice will become a habit."[9] In sports, Sterner emphasizes that "repeating a particular motion sixty times a day over twenty-one days will form a new habit that will become ingrained in your mind. The sixty repetitions needn't be done all at once but can be broken up into, say, six sets of ten or two sets of thirty during the day."[10] This discipline is exemplified in the practice habits of Stephen Curry of professional basketball fame. How does he land a shot, often from seemingly impossible range and position? How does he rack up incredulous statistics in three-point shooting and from the free-throw line? Well, he probably goes beyond the average 60 repetitions; perhaps he doubles it. Practice. Practice. What about 180 repetitions? Practice. Practice. Practice. No doubt, Curry goes above and beyond. That's how hard he works. Curry encourages young people, "If you take time to realize what your dream is and what you really want in life—no matter what it is, whether it's sports or in other fields—you have to realize that there is always work to do, and you want to be the hardest working person in whatever you do, and you put yourself in a position to be successful."[11] Curry said NO MATTER WHAT he puts in the hours with 200% effort. He aims for the top, does not quit, and takes his team to the end. Practice and repetition is the key to developing and getting better at anything.

Attending a Catholic private school did not help my practicing schedule. Classes started a little after 7:00 am and ended a little after 4:00 pm. I had thirteen subjects to study in elementary school: English Grammar, English Spelling, English Composition, English Literature, Science, Math, Social Studies, Religion, Filipino Language, Music/ Art, Home Economics, Physical Education, and Character Education. Extracurricular activities such as clubs and student council were also incorporated into an already-packed day. The little free time in between was designated for getting some homework done. Practicing the piano had to be relegated to an after-school, off-campus activity. I was usually home by 4:30 pm if I did not attend any club meetings. I grew up at a time when the family ate supper together, around 5:30 pm. That was the rule, no exception! Daddy sat at the head of the table. We talked about our day over rice, fish, and vegetables. After supper, a few more minutes would suffice to finish homework. Then, just like clockwork and without further chit-chat with Mama or Daddy, I launched into the practice ritual as expected, not a single word of protest, not even a hint of feeling wiped out from the entire day.

We had neighbors who did not have televisions, so you could expect them to be watching from outside one of the windows. Such rituals happened across neighborhoods. We, inside the house and fortunate enough to have a television, made sure not to block their views. It probably sounds creepy to have folks outside your window peering into your living room, but such was the Filipino culture. It's an unspoken understanding among neighbors. But because of the conservatory practices, my routine drastically changed. The television downstairs had to be moved upstairs so my younger sisters, Noemi and Loida, could finish their homework or study and watch some TV afterwards. Cousins joined them occasionally.

Downstairs, Daddy would position himself at his super-sized dark olive green square desk to read *The Manila Times*.

Why Daddy would sit through all the hours of torture when he was, in fact, musically illiterate, I never understood. He had his routine to which he adhered with conscientious compulsion. He would read the newspaper each morning, and what he couldn't get to, he caught up in the early evening. Every section, beginning with the headlines, then to world news, local news, to economic and society pages, from sports to the obituaries, column by column. He folded the paper accordingly with utmost care and punctuated rhythm. He would read almost the entire paper, nearly all, except the funnies. Daddy believed they were a total waste of time. He would have a few strong words for any grandchild caught thumbing through what he called garbage reading. Somehow, I managed on many occasions to steal the comic strips to follow the adventures of Beetle Bailey, Nancy, Blondie, Peanuts, and Mickey Mouse.

Practice and repetition is the key to developing and getting better at anything.

Daddy didn't know Bach from Beethoven or discern a wrong note, even if you deliberately banged the dissonant note fifty times. Just the same, he supervised my practice hours. His venerable presence alone was enough to command the kind of hushed behavior reserved for the library. One day, Mama confided that for Daddy, sitting at his desk and listening to me practice was what made him happy. I have only a few remembrances of Daddy coming home from work. I believe he retired when I was about seven years old. It made sense to me why he had all the time in the world to patrol my practice like a sentry. Mama, on the other hand, did not sit or watch. But she listened, for sure! She would be taking care of the other children or attending to household affairs, but there was never a doubt that her trained ears would hear every wrong note and every nuance of each piece. She was the real critic.

The practice ritual commenced only after I had closed every window on the first floor of the house. This was not your average-sized window. We're talking about a house in a tropical region that's built with heat and humidity in mind. Cross-ventilation was necessary. Screened non-glass windows surrounded the house to allow the wind to breeze through from one side to the other in all directions. There were four large windows to where the piano was situated. I had to slide four rectangular wooden window panels into position to completely close off each window. It's like installing hurricane shutters, but from the inside! The regimen was carried out with obsessive-compulsive precision and began after dinner every night. I was sure our neighbors appreciated the effort. I can only imagine the possible ruckus and complaining among them had I neglected this prerequisite to practice time.

Closing the windows was my idea. I refused to practice until every part of the window had been sealed, at least to buffer some of the noise that I knew would travel throughout the close-knit neighborhood. I was not sure why I felt compelled to close the windows, whether it was because of self-consciousness or simply a sense of duty. I worried that the kind of practice I did would probably be an intrusion into their homes. So, while families gathered next door or across the street around their television, eager to catch the new American shows that made their way to Southeast Asia, I practiced. Slightly frustrated that I was going to miss, again, the latest episode of *Bonanza* and the Cartwright family on their Ponderosa Ranch or wonder what's up with the cute astronaut in *I Dream of Jeannie*, I practiced. No way to record the shows back then. That was my life. I can still imagine the disappointment of our TV-less neighbors who, for no fault of their own, had to give up the same shows that I had to relinquish. I send them my deepest apologies for putting up the window shutters.

Practicing the piano would go on until close to 10:00 pm, Monday through Friday, except on Wednesdays. Wednesday was lesson day. I was approved for early dismissal from school to attend my weekly two-hour piano lesson. Mama and I did not get home till 7:00 pm on those days. Practicing on Wednesday was a short hour and a half, just enough to review what I learned that day.

The conservatory day was practically all day Saturday, from 9:00 am to 3:30 pm. You had to factor in the commute. I managed to fill the time between my sight singing class and theory class and during other breaks with more practice. Saturdays also found me accompanying concerto rehearsals. If I was not practicing my concertos, my teacher assigned me to accompany someone else's concerto. After a long day, I was grateful that I did not practice on Saturday night. A girl had to squeeze some time to recoup from the long, grueling week. I was more than delighted to skip Saturday's practice. Sunday was spent at church. It started with a Sunday school class, followed by the worship service with me accompanying at the piano. Our big family Sunday lunch was always special. This was the day we usually ate chicken, one chicken for an extended family. Then we rushed back to church for choir practice and youth groups till 4:00 pm. You might assume that I had the rest of the weekend off; the week ended on Sunday evening with practice from 7:00-9:00 pm, unless I was playing for church vesper services. Sadly, there was no rest on the Sabbath. How ironic!

It became obvious that while having been prodded by my parents and grandfather to practice diligently, I, and only I, decided to subscribe to this lifestyle. Long, lonely hours of practicing stared at me each night, sometimes gawking, daring to outface me, but I brazenly embraced back. I was ever mindful of the sacrifices necessary to pursue excellence, success, and fame. What seemed so mind-boggling was the fact that when I tried to tally up the hours spent at the piano, I wondered what other worthwhile or, better yet, fun things those hours could have been used for. Imagine the lost time spent away from family! Imagine the lost time that could have simply been devoted to being a kid. Occasionally, I dwell on the "what ifs." The pursuit of excellence could be a lonely road. This is also true of the marathoner, the Olympic gymnast, or a world-class swimmer.

In *Strength and Conditioning for Sports Performance*, Jeffries and Moody explain that "The objective of every athlete is to perform at his/her maximum level on competition day."[12] How does it happen? The athlete envisions the end goal of winning and decides to devote the time and dedication to prepare for sports performance, to submit the body and the mind to an extensive training schedule, balanced with rest periods, with the combination of strength and conditioning training for speed and agility development. The depth of the discipline is sometimes difficult for an average person to quantify. However, the single focus to win, to claim the gold medal, the gold cup, or the gold trophy, drives athletes to press on, to take the challenge to the end. Taylor, in *The Disciplined Life,* explains the sacrifice, "A willingness to undertake the labor involved in becoming disciplined is the first step in achieving our desires."[13]

One of the most impressive displays of athleticism was that of Nadia Comeneci during the 1976 Olympics gymnastics competition. The world, intrigued by the raw brilliance of Comeneci's star power, happily welcomed the talent and dedication of the child sports prodigy. I was glued to the television. She was a seriously shy teenager but rock solid, consistently superb in her delivery, and outscoring every competitor with her perfect 10s. The performances bore the signature of devotion to discipline. Her riveting execution became the measure of the standard of her sport. But that did not come easily. What propelled her to greatness in her youth was her submission to discipline, good habits, and sacrifices. Athletes and artists—their lives mirror each other in shooting for their goals and in how they dedicate themselves to practice!

Dedication to practice is a non-negotiable commodity in an artist's or athlete's quest for success. The discipline to practice

Dedication to practice is a non-negotiable commodity in an artist's or athlete's quest for success. The discipline to practice becomes your friend, but it comes with yet another challenge—endurance.

becomes your friend, but it comes with yet another challenge—endurance. Endurance is the ability to withstand pressure to finish what you started. It is what carries you through the rough times and what gets you to the other side.

Endurance was a lesson I learned by trial and error, or shall I say, by correcting bad habits. I did not set out intentionally to set up an endurance training agenda. After all, I wasn't an athlete!

I enjoyed practicing. I tackled multiple exercises to build finger strength and endurance. Developing good technique was a worthy endeavor. But something became problematic in the long run. I did not realize that to sustain the long hours of practice, my entire body must also be aligned with the mind. To only accede to a "when there's a will, there's a way" mentality would be lacking. Practicing must be sustainable with good endurance-building habits. In my uninformed and casual approach to practicing, I did not, in the least bit, consider that, perhaps, practicing the piano could be something much more than the finger bravura or the mental exercise of identifying the form, key structures, and chord progressions or the memorization of music. It requires attention to the vigorous physical exertion of the upper body, the shoulders, arms, hands, and fingers. It is a total body workout that calls for strong core muscles and the alignment of the spine, pelvis, hips, and legs. It takes complete conditioning from head to toe to play the piano and, especially, to build endurance for a successful performance. Longer music pieces require both mental and physical tenacity to be able to complete what could be a relatively taxing performance because of the sheer length of the piece.

I learned quickly that if I did not have the right kind of chair for practice, I would develop back and leg problems. The piano benches I used when I was a child at home or during a performance were of standard height. Not one chair was suitable for my petite frame and height. Because the chair was not high enough for me to sit on to reach a comfortable playing position for my arms and hands, I figured out I had to pile up three or four piano books on the piano bench to raise my "seat," quite primitive, when I think about it now. When piano books weren't enough to solve the height dilemma, I would grab a few of Mama's hymnals and stack them up to reach the right height for me. Unfortunately, the hymnals were only about half the size of my bottoms, so I had to cope with a tough balancing act on the bench. Alas, hymnals were not the preferred method to increase height. I fell off the hymnals a few times, suffered through some embarrassing moments, and some painful misalignment of my butt, thigh,

Practice must be sustainable with good endurance-building habits.

legs, and back. I also found out that doing some warm-ups before practicing, like stretching the upper body, especially the shoulders and arms, helped ease subsequent aches from shoulder muscles after a long practice session.

For all the good habits, I also had habits that did not get corrected until they had already become, yes, bad habits. One of them was the unnecessary repeated motion of the wrists, something that I might have copied off another pianist at a competition because it looked emotive and cool. I also used to tense up my wrist and fingers and play with a banging sound. My teacher addressed these quickly so I could break the bad habits that would hinder my steady progress. Posture was another problem for me. I tended to slouch on the bench when I played. So my piano teacher from when I was ten till about sixteen had me sit on a special Yamaha piano practice bench she owned, with a fairly small square seat and a chair back. Just by the construction of the chair and the adjustable seat to achieve the desired height level, it became easier to play with my spine straight and my shoulders straight and wide, perpendicular to my spine. I found my sweet spot, just the right height.

It was truly a magical chair, I thought. The chair helped with endurance. I did not know that I was capable of practicing for hours and hours until I played on that bench. I could practice long hours because I kept my posture in the correct position and alignment; I was neither too low nor too high at the piano because the seat was adjustable. And more importantly, I did not tire easily. There was not a bench like that anymore when I came to America.

Serendipitously, I ended up acquiring Yamaha practice chairs about 28 years ago without purchasing them. I spotted them at a Florida wholesale piano dealership. They sat in an inconspicuous back room, old, dirty, and forgotten. The piano store sold used Yamaha pianos from Asia. The chairs came with one of the large piano shipments from abroad. The owner did not know what to do with them. But he did notice my giddiness when I discovered the chairs in the back of the store. I had not seen this type of chair since I was 16. Suddenly, I felt like a little girl, thrilled like the first time I met a similar chair in Manila, one that was perfect for my height. The owner most definitely sensed my penchant for the benches, so he gladly gave them away—free of charge.

He said he could not sell them. The chairs came with several Yamaha uprights and grand pianos from Japan. They were not in mint condition but still solid and functional. Being gifted one bench would have felt like I hit the jackpot. But I lucked out in a big way, not just one, but three altogether! The dealer, who got a dose of my childhood stories about practicing and who keenly observed my attachment to his chairs, gave me two identical chairs with backs and another bench without a back. The chairs came with the original glossy black paint to match the black polished finish of Yamaha pianos. A burgundy-colored material covered the thinly padded seats. Who would have thought that I would ever coincidentally come across the chairs of my childhood during my college teaching career?

Whipple and Eckardt noted, "To achieve the highest

quality of life in all of its various pursuits, including endurance training and racing, you must cultivate a purposeful and thoughtful investment in the process rather than just the outcome."[14] I always thought that just as my teacher's chair was one of the most purposeful investments I was able to utilize to develop endurance and strength, the newly-discovered chairs, in turn, will help my students likewise. Well, where are these chairs now? I left one bench with the back in my teaching studio at the university so my piano students can enjoy the benefits of correct height and posture when playing the piano. The other bench I kept at home for my own personal practice time. The third bench became the travel performance bench, just in case the benches elsewhere were inadequate. The poor chairs are all worn out and need a new varnish. But like drill sergeants at Camp Discipline, they dutifully serve their purpose well. I do not want to part with them.

Steiner articulates, "Everything in life worth achieving requires practice. In fact, life itself is nothing more than one long practice session, an endless effort to refine our motions. When the proper mechanics of practice are understood, the task of learning something new becomes a stress-free experience of joy and calmness, a process which settles all areas in your life and promotes proper perspective on all of life's difficulties."[15] It is the dedication to practice that bears good fruit

It is the dedication to practice that bears good fruit by eliminating stress during the performance.

by eliminating stress during the performance. You come to a live performance with the confidence that you've given it all you've got. You've done your homework. You are armed with preparedness, precision, and a plan. Your

Dedication to practice eliminates stress on one end and builds endurance on the the other.

mental focus is on high alert to tackle any challenge that might still sneak in—that's why it's called live performance. Dedication to practice eliminates stress on one end and builds endurance on the other. Endurance is the companion of discipline to take a task to the end. It's what helps you react proactively to surprises along the way, no matter what the challenge may be.

Though I draw a similar comparison between athlete and artist, I can only imagine what athletes have to subject their minds and bodies to build the highest level of stamina and endurance. I am amazed at the kind of endurance training they are willing to take because it's the product of their endurance training that will kick in during critical moments to win the game. One of my favorite movies is *Miracle,* the story of the 1980 United States men's Olympic hockey team that won the gold medal. They had a tough coach. The scene that I play over and over again is the part when the coach, after a game that ended in a tie, took the team back into the arena to skate back and forth from one end of the rink to the other for an extended period, even playing in the dark after the rink manager had turned off the lights. The players began to fall down, one by one, from sheer exhaustion. The coach was trying to make a point about unity, but the exercise was a strategy for building endurance.

"How do you get to Carnegie Hall?" The punchline is "Practice. Practice. Practice." It takes an enormous measure of discipline and endurance. Carnegie Hall is a rental concert venue. Anyone who can pay the cost can play at Carnegie. There are many school choirs, youth orchestras, and artists from all music and art genres who play at Carnegie Hall, yet only a small number of elite artists who are already famous, either by winning competitions or by sustaining successful performing careers, actually "play Carnegie" and get paid for doing so. Perhaps a more appropriate question is, "What is your Carnegie Hall?" What is your ultimate goal? What is the greatest achievement you're reaching for? How will you get there? Consider arming yourself with discipline and endurance.

3 | PREPARING FOR THE UNEXPECTED

The first time I had a light-bulb moment of how discipline and endurance training pay off in the long run was when I was eleven. Mrs. Stella Goldenberg Brimo, my piano teacher then of a little over a year, presented me at a premiere recital, a large-scale concert to introduce the young prodigy to the public. I was in fifth grade. Schoolwork had become more demanding. I also was class president and entered elocution contests. Preparation for the significantly substantial concert program called for much prioritizing and even more discipline. Mama was also pregnant in her third trimester, approaching the concert date. She got tired more easily, and her tummy appeared to be ballooning out each week. Yet she accompanied me to the lessons and rehearsals just the same.

The repertoire was extensive: The *Mozart Piano Concerto in A Major K. 414* in three movements to start the program, then followed by three piano solos, and concluded with the *Mendelssohn Piano Concerto in G Minor*. The Manila Symphony Orchestra was contracted to accompany the two concertos. I had already performed with them earlier at a Young Artists' Competition Concert. So I was looking forward to performing again with familiar faces. Daddy asked Uncle Mel, still single and living in Indianapolis, to help pay for the orchestra and other recital expenses, including the rental fee for the Fleur de Lis Auditorium at St. Paul's College, Manila. It made sense to schedule the recital there. I attended the St. Paul's College Conservatory of Music, and the stage was big enough to hold an orchestra of 20-30 members. The fees included the rehearsals for both concertos and the actual performance. The first concerto was from the Classical style period. The orchestral members numbered about 20 for the Mozart ensemble. But the second concerto was from the Romantic period and required ten additional players. I did not have the slightest clue what a huge burden Uncle Mel had to take on to make the recital happen. It was an ambitious and expensive program.

The Mozart *Concerto* started with a strong ensemble between the orchestra and the soloist. The concerto was a 26-minute piece in three movements. I got through the first two movements without a hitch. I remember calming down my nerves early on in the piece even though we ambitiously led off with a concerto, of all things to start with. I was enjoying the performance. I was approaching the cadenza of the third movement (a rondeau movement). Translation to non-music people: I was almost towards the end of the entire concerto, with three minutes left, when at 23:00, a performer's worst nightmare swept in without warning. A mental block! What was probably only a matter of 18 seconds in real-time, for me, transpired in extremely slow motion, an eternity.

Entering a section where I played solo as the orchestra faded out, I was supposed to play a modulatory chord progression signaling the return to the home key of A Major. The concerto was nearing the end. After playing the two-note upbeat of the passage, I hesitated and, for a few seconds, doubted the key I landed on. Instead of proceeding, I switched keys and played another two-note upbeat, the pattern that led to a similar section earlier in the movement, at 21:00. That didn't sound right either. Thrown off by the misstep, I played the two-note pattern, shifting back and forth between that of the key of A Major and that of the key of E Major, trying to decide which chord progression I should follow—the key which would take me to the end of the concerto. I did not stop. I kept trying to find my way back to get to the end. Thank goodness the orchestra was not playing with me. I had the luxury of a solo section to recover from or cover my own mistake.

While I was idiotically alternating the short motivic pattern between the two prospective keys of A Major or E Major, I noticed that the conductor, with both hands still up in the air, did his best to hold back the orchestra. All eyes were on the conductor for directions. Well, he made some subtle hand signals, trying to get the players' attention to get ready to come back and join me at the right place in the piece. I briefly glanced over to see how he was going to respond to the chaos that was about to explode. I saw him mouthing an instruction. He was planning to catch me on whichever key I landed. I thought for a second, *Thank you, Lord, this fine gentleman had my back, after all. No worries here.* Either we proceed correctly to end the piece or go back to the 21:00 point; he was going to meet me there. Had I gone further back to the beginning of the third movement, he was slightly motioning with his left hand to get ready to turn back their pages to a particular letter section on the score. The instrumentalists assigned to turn pages motioned forward toward their music stands to get ready to turn back their pages, just in case I did decide to start all over again. What a suspenseful 18 seconds! Taylor gives sound advice on this kind of situation, "Learn to turn into good advantage the unscheduled twist of events which throws your well-laid plans into confusion . . . The finest self-discipline is seen, not in rigidity, but in resiliency."[1]

I don't know how I did it, but I did it. Somehow, my trustworthy fingers, guided by my trained ears and memory work, recalled where they were supposed to go and chose the correct path toward the conclusion of the concerto. I got out of that bind, all right! I summoned every ounce of pluck and preparation in my playbook. I was going to take this to the end, no matter what! Gordon aptly describes the process, "Know that every successful performer has had to call upon mental teeth-gritting at some point. Moreover, getting tough with yourself at the right moment often leaves you feeling good about yourself because you rose to the challenge when the going was rough."[2]

I could hardly hold back the tears as I acknowledged the thunderous applause after the concerto ended. I was taught not to apologize or show any sign of a weak moment in any performance. It was crucial to exude the utmost professionalism even under great duress—the show must go on, forget the mistakes, focus, and move on. As I look back to that time in 1967, I think of three things: First of all, what a tremendous pressure on a young girl to even have played one concerto, much less two major concertos! Second, how did I get out of that dilemma alive? Did I rely on my developing musicianship skills, or was it the presence of mind, or maybe it was just pure luck? Third, unless you were familiar with that particular Mozart *Concerto*, no one in the audience noticed my anguish during the blip and a near-disaster of performance in the last movement of said concerto because I kept on playing. Of course, my teacher and Mama knew!

I remember going back to the green room after I made a few curtain calls. Mrs. Brimo and Mama came to greet me behind the curtain. I became hysterical. I was sobbing and, true to form, the prima donna that I was, vehemently announced, "There is no way I'm going back on that stage again. The concert's over!" I was having a full-blown tantrum. I didn't quite understand the calm reaction of those around me backstage. My teacher reassured me that it went fine, that I astoundingly recovered well, and that we still had the rest of the program to finish. Oh yes, I still had to play short pieces of Beethoven, Schumann, and Debussy. We're not even into the intermission yet! And remind me again, another concerto. All too much for a kid! Meanwhile, Mama was doing the mom thing, rubbing my back and trying to soothe and quiet my agitated state. Again, this happened so long ago that I don't remember anymore of what else transpired in that room, except that I was most definitely throwing a fit.

However, in a matter of minutes, reason prevailed. I mustered enough courage to face the audience who, in most likelihood, did not even have a clue about the mishap. I went back on stage after the out-of-body experience backstage, now surprisingly composed, to finish the first half of the program. I played the solo set, three contrasting pieces that pulled the audience into a more intimate setting compared to the dazzle of the piano concerto. My teacher and my mother watched from the stage right wing, more relieved than anyone else. They joined forces on crisis management. They alone witnessed the meltdown.

During the 15-minute intermission that followed, the stage was rearranged to accommodate the ten additional orchestra members for the Romantic orchestra set-up of the Mendelssohn *Concerto*. Semi-recovered from the momentary mental breakdown in the green room, I noticed from a window a group of orchestral players hanging outside. The players were chatting, and a few were smoking, waiting for the second half of the concert to begin. The orchestra was about to perform with me the longer Mendelssohn *Concerto*, the lone piece of the second half. My perfectionist self would not easily let go of what had just happened in the first half. I imagined the snafu of the Mozart *Concerto* provided good fodder for gossip among the musicians. Yes, I was paranoid, too. Nevertheless, the show must go on.

The Mendelssohn *Concerto* has always been one of my favorites to this day. I listened to Andre Watts' performance when I wrote this section. It is rousing, rhythmically driving, with beautiful soaring melodies characteristically Mendelssohn's and brilliant virtuosic running passages, manageable even for an 11-year-old. Mendelssohn's style is not overly dramatic; instead, it is restrained and march-like, yet it has the sentimental flavor of the Romantic idiom. The first movement began with flair. The additional orchestral players certainly added spectacle in volume and fullness of tone to the competitive nature of a concerto, soloist versus orchestra. The mental glitch in the first half of the concert was now a distant memory. It's time for a full recovery. I can do this. I was going to have my happy ending. What mattered was that I ended well.

The concerto, quite honestly, was exhilarating to play. My tiny fingers vigorously flew across the keys and matched the rhythmic drive of the orchestral accompaniment. The first movement roared from the onset, with screaming octaves, multiple scale passages in all the minor forms, the dreaded scales at the interval 6ths apart, and an assortment of arpeggiated patterns interspersed with a contrasting simple lyrical second theme. The intensity of the piece barreled through towards the end of the movement, as if leading into a definitive ending with a strong cadence, only to be halted by an orchestral coda that signaled the movement was transitioning seamlessly into the next movement.

An unforgettable moment of the performance occurred at the beginning of the second movement. The extremely expressive melody in E Major is one of my all-time best-loved Romantic melodies. It was also Papa's favorite passage that I played. Papa was a jokester, a truly funny man. When he's telling a story, I find myself waiting each time for some kind of punchline. Some of his stories were about Bach, Beethoven, and Chopin. Before I received any formal training in theory and history at the conservatory, Papa had already introduced me to the intriguing lives of the great masters who penned great works of art. He bought me a thick biography book of composers. I ravaged through page after page, fascinated by the complex nature of their upbringing, education, and relationships. Several were child prodigies. For a man with only a sixth-grade level of education, without any formal training on any instrument, Papa was knowledgeable about history, languages, the arts, and music. He played the guitar with a classical bent by ear. During a few occasions when he sat down to listen to me practice, Papa would ask me to play Mendelssohn's second movement so he could hum along as I played it. His toothy smile was my reward each time. To this day, the memory brings tears to my eyes each time I play the second movement.

This is how I recall this portion of the concert. The piano began the second movement alone, with a short ascending line introduction, much like asking a question. Then the orchestra quickly answered with the first statement of the ethereal melody. The piano countered with the same melody, solo again, slowly expanding itself into phrases of aural charm and heartfelt sentiment. When I got to this part, for a split second that my concentrated train of thought would allow me while performing such a highly concentrated task, indulgence stepped in. I leisurely thought of Papa and his love for the tune as I proceeded to enjoy its beauty as well. I continued to the middle part of the movement. The sheer elegance of the pining melody intricately woven into the genius orchestration was more than enough to propel me to play with greater abandon, a common reaction of a performer to a Romantic melody. I could be easily lost, no doubt, in the moment.

And then, I heard it! It came piercing through the hushed, gentle dialogue between the soloist and orchestra. The familiar cough borne out of a long streak of habitual cigarette smoking, but, perhaps, also a cough brought on by a slight anxiety for his daughter's arduous and challenging task, still a few more minutes to complete. Papa coughed, not once, but at least three times. I heard him, during our mutually favored second movement of the concerto, as if we had set up a meeting of minds, a very public yet private conversation between father and daughter towards the end of the evening, courtesy of Mendelssohn. While some would call the coughing a distraction, I would venture to say that it was for this serendipitous moment that I practiced a lot. Gordon explains it this way. In "preparing for your performance, remember that virtually every performer comes to the point of having to use plain old-fashioned discipline to keep the process going."[3]

He goes on to punctuate the importance that "a movement or pattern needs to be repeated over and over within the period of a few minutes to impress the detail on

I knew the music so well I allowed myself a little indulgence.

your consciousness and work toward an automatic response. We tire of repeated patterns very quickly, both mentally and physically, sometimes after only a few repetitions. We do need to repeat certain patterns many times just to understand them or to organize them in our thinking and movements. We do need to master the physical responses we must call upon in our performance."[4]

I was able to handle the so-called distraction because I mastered a physical and mental response to keep on going, no matter what. I practiced hard so that I could handle any distractions or surprises. A tender moment of connecting with Papa in another realm was worth the challenge of a little intrusive thought. I knew the music so well I allowed myself a little indulgence. I was already playing with abandon anyway. The German poet Friedrich von Schiller puts it this way, "Only those who have the patience to do difficult things perfectly will acquire the skill to do difficult things easily."[5]

Call it a distraction. I call it a connection. Music, with its ability to elicit a strong emotional response, transported me instantaneously to a warmhearted thought of my father. Of course, that was not the right time and place to daydream. How did I do it? I had to be so prepared and so well-rehearsed to indulge in a split-second diversion, to momentarily step out of mental focus and trust my fingers to do the work. Confidence is an intangible reward for doing the hard work.

This tops my father-daughter unforgettable memories of

all time. The Mendelssohn *Concerto* will remain dearest to my heart because, during that live performance, I felt closest to Papa. I went on to finish the entire concerto without any incident or drama, unlike the Mozart *Concerto*. Each detail of the evening is embedded in my aging mind. After that night, having performed the Mozart and Mendelssohn concertos in one evening, I became a bona fide concert pianist. It was November 19, 1967. I endured the demands and surprises of a full-length concert with a full orchestra that day. A few weeks later, Mama faced a different kind of endurance test. My baby brother, Gedeon, was born. My family was ecstatic. We have a boy in the family, finally! It was going to be a merrier Christmas than usual.

The responsibility to develop, use, and share the talent to inspire others, at

> Music, with its ability to elicit a strong emotional response, transported me instantaneously to a warmhearted thought of my father.

the very least, can be a way to make our complex social interactions with one another pleasurable. Paterson stresses, "The purpose for your life is to put your God-given gifts to work for good in your generation and in your sphere of influence. In putting your giftedness to work for God's purposes, and in moving from self-centeredness to Christ-centeredness, you will experience a radiant, totally *alive* life."[6] I was content playing the piano just for myself. I enjoyed the long hours of study and solitude. I

Confidence is an intangible reward for doing the hard work.

was oblivious to my potential for a high-impact capacity to inspire through my performance and to do good in my generation. The life-giving impact of our connectivity and community was lost on me. I was a shy child, quiet and serious. I did not mind being alone. On the contrary, Papa was friendly and popular in his workplace, a radio and television network. Mama's social circles extended beyond family and friends to area churches' women's groups, neighbors, and strangers. Daddy was a respected elder in the church and the community. They were social butterflies. They encouraged us to make connections and develop relationships with people. They believed in performing acts of service and sharing your talent with others. They regarded that talent should not go to waste. Hiding it under a bushel, definitely not, they would say! Perform as much as you can. Inspire others. Bless others.

Papa entered me in a radio singing competition when I was five. Why? I have no idea. He thought maybe I could sing, but no luck there. A television talent show was next when I was six. This time, I played the piano, and I won. You can say I began entertaining people at a young age. Maybe I did inspire other young kids to acquire some kind of music education. I probably prompted a few potential stage moms to push their children to take piano lessons. I performed here, there, and everywhere. By age nine, I began my church career by playing for worship services. My home church was on the next parallel street across our house. The siblings and I used a shortcut through the yard of Auntie Doris, the oldest of Papa's six younger sisters. It led straight to the church's back door. I alternated with Auntie Encar, Papa's youngest sister, playing for the Sunday morning services. If that were not enough, I gradually eased into playing the opening songs for Wednesday night's grown-up Bible study and Thursday night prayer meetings. I would come in and play in the beginning, then run back to the house using the shortcut to resume practicing, then run back for the closing song, if any. The church gig afforded me the rare opportunity over the

The responsibility to develop, use, and share the talent to inspire others, at the very least, can be a way to make our complex social interactions with one another pleasurable.

years to practically learn and memorize the music and the lyrics of much of the American hymnal. Back in the day, we sang all the stanzas.

Because we were dedicated church members, that alone multiplied our human connection. Mama and Daddy were hospitable. We oftentimes had guests, family, friends, and church folks over, a bit too much for a bashful girl. I cannot remember a day when I wasn't asked to play something, at least one piece, for various visitors or at small and large family gatherings. I was taught that every opportunity to play would help me conquer stage fright, though I don't remember ever having been paralyzed by such fear. I was always good to go. I had a repertoire ready for any occasion. I did not mind the fuss. I was beginning to relish the attention. Playing in our living room when all the windows were open meant I was playing for someone else's pleasure. It's like being on call—to perform.

Our church joined four other churches every fifth Sunday of the month for an area-wide "singspiration," an old word for a hymn singing worship service, a short message, and choral numbers from the representing choral group of each congregation. It was also customary for the church choirs to go caroling each Christmas season. Daddy got a call from one director, not ours, asking if our family would be willing to host their choir. Christmas caroling by a Filipino choir translated to 1) a group of 15-25 descending to your house, 2) the group arriving anytime after 7:00 pm, 3) the host family serving refreshments, which could range anywhere from sandwiches and hot cocoa to soups like chicken *arroz caldo* (soup), to the traditional Filipino fare of *pancit* (rice noodles) and *lumpia* (spring rolls).

I was only nine years old, but I could still walk anyone today through the events of one evening embedded in the deep crevices of my memory. I was already asleep. I heard a commotion in the street. At first, I thought I was dreaming. But I heard them loud and clear. No, it wasn't a dream. I was awakened from a deep slumber by voices, accompanied by a guitar, singing the jolly, fast-moving "Ang Pasko Ay Sumapit" (Christmas Has Arrived), a Tagalog Christmas song, from outside my second-floor bedroom window.

Still half asleep, I turned around to check the clock. It was 11:30 pm, almost midnight. What in the world? The group changed up the tempo and began to sing "Silent Night" and "Hark the Herald Angels Sing" as they processed into our living room, right beneath my bedroom. I knew what was about to happen. I had a momentary, rebellious, sassy conversation with myself in my head that I had no desire to entertain a traveling vocal army who interrupted my beauty sleep in the middle of the night. I made up my mind: I was not going downstairs to play for the caroling strangers.

They barreled through their repertoire of carols in English and Tagalog. While they warbled, I so wished upon the Star of Bethlehem that night—no—I prayed and begged the Christ Child to grant my wish that I would be left alone to sleep in heavenly peace. My revolting heart wanted to win this battle! Then I heard Mama's sweet voice halfway up the staircase, calling out my name, not once, but four times, to hurry downstairs. I pretended to sleep. But, of course, the urging did not stop. I tried my best to stand my ground. But my temporary, contrary self swiftly surrendered to the usual compliant child. I grudgingly moseyed down the stairs in my pajamas and went straight to the piano. The living and dining rooms resembled a marketplace. Some were drinking hot cocoa. Others cued in line for the pimento cheese sandwiches. Mama was mumbling a few words to me when I walked by her but I did not listen. I was not a happy camper. I ambled into whatever narrow zig-zag space was available, passing through sweet folks with their *oohs* and *ahs*, a few already applauding, appreciative of the emerging concert. I did not make a scene, but I did not smile either. I performed a short Chopin piece and another short Christmas hymn arrangement. You couldn't tell the begrudging attitude with my brilliant performance. But there was no way I was going to play "We Wish You A Merry Christmas," either. It turned out the choir had the last word on that.

The 1984 movie *Amadeus*, depicting the life of child prodigy Wolfgang Amadeus Mozart, featured a scene with little Mozart playing the harpsichord to a royal audience. Quickly afterward, his father propped up Mozart to play the violin. Not quite the same audience I had that Christmas night. But the Mozart scene reminded me of the many occasions I was displayed to any random audience with the belief that the more I played on the spot at times, the better I would be able to handle the pressure of a live concert performance. Perform. Perform. Perform.

The idea of performing and demonstrating my talent to inspire others was challenging to grasp. One thing for sure: I did not want to be like a trained street monkey, playing at the behest of its trainer. Nor was I a jukebox either, ready to spit out any song for a quarter at the push of a button. I certainly had my issues in this regard. Although I was pretty comfortable playing in public, my introverted self oftentimes clashed with the demands of an extroverted performance and the constant expectation to execute. This has become a lifelong struggle for me. I have learned to be an extrovert, but I certainly am not a social party animal by any means. •

I had no lofty goal of being an inspiration to anybody. My ambition was to display my talent for self-glory, for the applause and the attention, for money. It was only after I became a follower of Christ that I began a deliberate process of peeling away my pride and self-centeredness to discover a better way of shifting focus away from myself and instead, pointing every day to the One who is the Giver of all good gifts. It's a hard lesson to learn when you grow up thinking you're the best thing that ever happened to your family and the Manila concert culture. But I learned it anyway, slowly but surely. And it changed my life. Pride is still an ongoing nemesis, but I can recognize and call it out in the context of knowing and acknowledging who God is and what He has done and continues to do for me. I also learned what false humility looks like.

Much of my work in teaching music revolved around demonstrating in a piano lesson how a piece is played, or in a theory class or a music appreciation course how music in history has been performed. I believe that a performing artist plays to the class to illustrate a point. I hope, at least, that the students find inspiration from the talent that I allowed to shine through me for the glory of God, and if my effort motivates them to be more dedicated to their craft, so much the better. As in the parable of the talents

> Pride is still an ongoing nemesis, but I can recognize and call it out in the context of knowing and acknowledging who God is and what He has done and continues to do for me.

or the bags of gold, depending on which Bible version you read, I would like to think that I am living a life that honors God, who calls me to do something with what I have been given. If, in the process, others are spurred on to do likewise, I count that as a blessing, my return on investment. Justin Miller, lead pastor of Real Life Christian Church, delivered an emphatic message about talents: "Focus on what is in front of you, on what you have . . . What are you doing with what God has given you . . . We live to pay it forward and to bring [God] a return because He is our Master and He is good. He has given us so much . . . It just makes sense that [God] want[s] a return on this investment."[7] It goes back to the parable of talents. When you're given a gift, you pass it on by investing and using your gift, and the gifting process goes on. The return on investment is reaped on multiple levels. Paterson adds, "Gifted musicians never feel better or have a greater sense of purpose and fulfillment than when they are engaged in the performance of their gift. This same combination of excellence, enjoyment, and giftedness exists for every type of talent or combination of talents."[8] This is what motivates me to endure the long hours of practicing to perform. A disciplined life fosters lifelong personal growth and development. It facilitates good stewardship of the gifts. Moreover, it prepares you for the unexpected.

4 | THE ROAD TO JUILLIARD

An extremely disciplined existence for me was a given. There weren't too many hours to juggle regular school work with an expectation to excel academically and practice at least five hours of piano daily. There were a few extracurricular activities to accommodate. No time was wasted watching TV or playing with the neighborhood kids. Learning skills that were essential for the concert world was a priority. Time management and efficiency became precious commodities. Life suddenly became hectic. As oblivious as I might have seemed to be about the future, I hopped onto a road that definitely was going somewhere.

By the age of ten, I learned proper dining etiquette. I read books with table-setting diagrams. Mama and I practiced at the dining table. I knew which fork or spoon to pick up at a formal dinner. I was taken back in time by a scene from the Leonardo DiCaprio movie *Titanic* when the young heroine, Rose, observed a young girl being strictly coached by her mother at the dinner table how to sit and eat properly with a mixture of grace, sensibility, and demureness. I became ambivalent watching the film segment. I wasn't sure whether to cry or get angry because I could identify with the little girl. Mama also trained me in proper conversational etiquette so that I could handle the numerous dinner parties in Manila's high society circles. I practiced the balance of being polite, engaging, listening, when to speak at the proper time, and how to address folks with their correct titles. Miss Manners would have been proud.

Papa, once in a while, would come into the picture. Papa worked for a Filipino radio and television station. He started as a driver and mechanic of the network's fleet of vehicles. He was later trained and promoted to become a newsreel cameraman. It was Papa who entered me in my first competition. I remember the stage, the stage curtain, the old-fashioned microphone, and lots of people milling around backstage in a live radio show. It was a chaotic and overwhelming scene for a little girl. I did not win the prize, but the experience became my rite of passage into the entertainment culture. Papa groomed me accordingly. Papa occasionally visited the sets in the TV station, his children in tow, to hang out with news broadcasters and actors. Our family attended the company Christmas parties. We marveled at the large-boxed gifts for the kids. Somehow, Papa managed to secure my guest appearances on live and taped TV shows. I met TV and movie celebrities, comedians, and professional musicians before I was ten. Thereafter, as a guest soloist in orchestra venues, I eased into the circles of the military, world-class musicians, dancers, artists, Philippine politicians, and even a U.S. ambassador. The whirlwind affair with the rich and famous sounds too unbelievable when I think about it today. It was a lifetime ago, in stark contrast to my present quieter and under-the-radar life as a wife, mother, professor, and pastor's wife.

To an impressionable child prodigy, the allure to embrace the magical, albeit overly protected world of concert galas, couture attire, and opportunities to meet high society patrons of the art was like being handed the candy jar. It brought the sweetest taste of unappeasable stardom. It fostered an intoxicating air of confidence brought by recognition and prestige at such a young age, far greater than being the top academic student in your private school. Who would not want to attend parties of the rich and powerful? To be invited to play a Bach or Mozart at a philanthropic ladies' afternoon tea! Who would not revel in taking center stage with an army of professional instrumentalists accompanying you? Imagine having had the backstage privilege to meet internationally renowned artists. Who would have refused a free new sequined or beaded concert attire, courtesy of one of Manila's fashion designers, who happened to be Daddy's family friend? I don't recall repeating an outfit, ever!

Lou (Lourdes), a childhood friend who now resides in Malaysia, and I were recently messaging each other. Lou recalled a memory when we were in upper elementary school of a concert I performed at the newly built Cultural Center of the Philippines, a prestigious music and art center in Manila. Our entire class of about 30 students, plus chaperones, attended. School-approved field trips back in the day included attending any one of my concerts in town.

Of course, I was oblivious to any of this. I only realized that my friends were in the audience when I came onto the stage to bow before moving towards the piano. You couldn't miss the sea of well-behaved parochial school girls clad in blue and white uniforms sitting together towards one side of the concert hall.

After all these years, Lou described in detail my concert dress that evening—that I wore a white lace dress with a ballooning skirt that reached just above the knee, one of my couture outfits. She reminisced how our classmates, upon entering the lobby, became so obsessed with the new red carpeted floor that a few girls took a roll on the plush pile for fun. I asked another friend, Espot (Esperanza), which particular classmate toppled over the floor. No one wanted to fess up on a group text message, and since it happened decades ago, no one could remember who instigated the gymnastics floor exercise-like shenanigan. But we suspected unanimously that it was probably Malooh (Marilou). My friends surely were a notorious bunch! Such was my young life—missing out on the simple pleasures of childhood, but a life that felt like being caught up in a slow-moving fantasy, à la Cinderella, without the wicked stepmother and stepsisters. But it was not a dream nor a fantasy. It was my reality! Success and acclaim came so readily, things many people can only dream of or place on a bucket list. The seemingly magical way of existence brought a stark contrast to an insanely real world of hard work, regimented lifestyle, and isolation. If there were not enough hours in the day for this kind of life, it's safe to say that something had to give. In other words, I had to forgo something or even several things. What did I sacrifice for the sake of fame and glory? Let me count the ways.

I remember the chattering of siblings, cousins, and other kids playing in the street. It could be a Filipino game of *tumbang preso*, a popular children's pastime of hitting empty tin cans with a slipper, or *patintero*, a Filipino version of tag with "passers" and "guards," or my favorite, *shatong*, a game that required counting, a short stick and a long stick, and some mean batting skills. Any of these after-school neighborhood rituals were how kids passed the time after homework and before supper. There would be 10-12 children, more on a few occasions, one minute laughing and cheering on their teams, the next minute, erupting into loud arguments. I could hear them from within the fortress of the living room, zoned for piano practice. I would occasionally look out the window, sometimes

To an impressionable child prodigy, the allure to embrace the magical, albeit overly protected world of concert galas, couture attire, and opportunities to meet high society patrons of the art was like being handed the candy jar.

ambivalent with the nagging question, "Why am I not out there with them?" I got annoyed at all the commotion they were creating, and still sometimes sad, if only for a second, wishing I could join the festivity without feeling guilty. As I grew older each year, I tried to convince myself that I was occupied with more noble pursuits, not some childish diversion. Over time, I learned the art of tuning out the yelling and the laughter. I eventually heard them as background noise. But who was I kidding?

I don't recall Papa watching sports on television, or much television for that matter, except during basketball season. He would catch a bit of his favorite team's games on TV late at night. I remember that he and Daddy loved boxing and the great Muhammad Ali, aka Cassius Clay. Bowling, however, was the favorite pastime among the uncles and aunts. I believe it could be the national sport of Filipinos. From whom I inherited my love for basketball and volleyball is still a mystery to me. After I got married, my husband, Eli, taught me to play catch, shoot baskets, and play tennis.

However, since there were not enough hours in a day, I was strictly forbidden to play sports in school or watch professional Filipino basketball games on TV in the late evenings. I would practice piano until 10:00 pm and hope that I would be allowed to catch the second half of the game or its final minutes, but alas, I would be sent to bed. This frustration became a nightly ritual. I would try to negotiate the privilege of a few minutes of mindless TV fare after a hard day's work in school, practice, and homework. But it was to no avail. I lived under two strict enforcers, Daddy and Mama. Only Papa empathized with me. Occasionally, he and I managed to outwit Daddy and Mama to enjoy a few minutes of basketball bliss. It was no different in school. I was not allowed to play volleyball or basketball.

Roller-skating was out of the question. The priority was to protect the ten little digits from any possible form of injury. The sacrifice to give up sports was paramount in the disciplined lifestyle of a performing musician.

But in retrospect, what I missed the most was not hanging out enough with my younger siblings and cousins, whether it was just sitting down to read together or playing silly street games. One thing we were encouraged to play a lot, only as a matter of practicality, was the game Scrabble. Daddy was convinced a word game would improve our English vocabulary, contrary to street play, which, according to him, would only lead us into trouble. The children heard this warning all the time. So we played Scrabble and other variations of the game we invented. Those were fond memories. Apart from that, the time we siblings spent together was few and far between. The situation was exacerbated when my younger sister Noemi, who was only eleven at the time, left Manila for Ontario, Canada, to live with an uncle and his wife. That was an Asian thing: send a child to live abroad, preferably with a relative, to get a better education or supposedly a better life. The children did not have any say in this. Adults made all the decisions, whether ill-advised or not well-informed. No consideration was given to whether the move would have psychological and emotional consequences on a child. It's a Filipino mentality.

Regret comes in hindsight. I wish I had spent time just to be around my baby sisters and brother more, being silly and mischievous, bantering, telling corny jokes, and telling lots of stories about ghosts and Filipino folklore scary creatures in the late afternoon and into the dark (the *multo*, *manananggal*, *aswang*, *tiktik*, *kapre*, and *tikbalang*). I wish we spent more time singing, laughing, and getting soaked in the tropical rain, tasting its sweet water droplets, running to the ubiquitous *sari-sari* store (convenience store) to buy candy and a sarsaparilla drink or, even better, Coca-Cola. I wish we fought like the children we were supposed to be, but also built friendships that were sown in our younger years, and hopefully blossoming to deep relationships into adulthood. I even missed the proverbial competition among us, like who was awarded the most number of merit cards each grading period or who got first prize in the elocution contest. I wish I could have chaperoned my younger siblings to anywhere they were supposed to be. I didn't have enough time to grow into the older sister I should have been.

These had all been lost in the quandary of migrating to a foreign land, America, the land of opportunity. I was the oldest child in my generation, the star of the family with a concert career. The road to Juilliard was almost inevitable. Needless to say, I believed an invisible wall might have been fortuitously built between me and my brother and sisters as if to set me apart from all the other children. My life and their life were oceans apart. My intuitive young self sensed an unspoken truth in my family: The other children were permitted to remain the kids that they were while I had to grow up, regrettably, at warp speed.

The Early Years

I experienced a level of education that cannot be encountered in the regular classroom. I tasted a degree of visual, aural, and sensory stimulation within music and art circles. It was so intense that even the rigor of study and discipline during my elementary and high school years would rank like child's play. It became crystal clear that I was, indeed, living in two worlds. In school, I was an academic overachiever, excelling in all subjects, playing intramural volleyball (I will explain in a later chapter), engaging in after-school dodgeball games, and participating in school-sponsored extracurricular activities. I was in talent shows and school plays. I played Saint Bernadette of Lourdes in a musical operetta. I led a group of my best friends in singing competitions at our school and our sister schools. I ran for student council and class office. I spent hours in group study and class projects. I was a member of several clubs, including the Eucharistic Crusade, the Glee Club, and the Geography Club. I was a contributor to the school paper, *L'Etincelle*. I also played the pump organ for Mass Monday through Friday in school before classes started. I was as visible as any student leader could be on campus. But when I left the school compound, I stepped into my alter ego—the budding musician with a tightly scheduled routine of weekly two-hour piano lessons, Saturday conservatory classes, weekly Friday night concert attendance and socializing, and, of course, rehearsing and concertizing.

Many children would have struggled with this kind of

pressure. It's a tough road to travel for anyone, let alone a young human. But once on the journey, one develops boldness and resilience to face the onslaught of high expectations for excellence and discipline. How is this lifestyle sustainable at all? Where does the support come from? There's a kind **Regret comes in hindsight.** of self-assured outlook that children develop when they're brought up feeling secure, loved, and deeply valued. Mama's dedication to me and my music career was a gift from the good Lord. I was so relieved she was not the typical dreaded stage mom. Yes, she was a stage mom in the sense that she accompanied me to all my lessons, auditions, and competitions. She arranged for the entire concert wardrobe and hairstyling. But Mama was likable and a people person. She was not demanding of others and not harsh on me. She did not hover. She did not threaten. She did not yell; well, what I meant was that she did not yell to embarrass me in public. We did not fight, well, not a lot. When we did, it was probably because of my prima donna attitude. I was the more sensitive type, moody, with a temperamental personality.

Mama was not the nagging kind, either. She was the least overbearing mother anyone could ever know. Mama was sweet and kind, not an attention-seeking diva. She was an extremely sensible musician and choir director, nurturing and with a deep well for sound and practical musical tips. Mama accompanied me to every lesson, class session, rehearsal, concert, and performance in my younger career. She was not in the best of health, but to me, she won the *Perfect Parent Attendance Award*. Mama was the other trained musician in the family, so her supportive role was most logical to the pragmatic tendencies my family embraced. Though Mama was an extrovert, she did not carry herself with an air of self-importance. I, on the other hand, was gaining more confidence and beginning to enjoy the much attention about me. Although I was reserved and aloof most of the time, my temperament was slowly emerging as intuitive but dominant.

So, who was the stage mom? I believe Mama just carried out her father's wishes. Perhaps it was Daddy who was the stage grandpa, if only by proxy. Daddy was certainly imposing. My grandfather was strict and controlling. He was also extremely organized. He strategized and directed my young life towards pursuing the music dream. I've often wondered whose dream it was. His or mine? Depending on what day it is, my answer fluctuates back and forth in

It became crystal clear that I was, indeed, living in two worlds.

trying to figure out what or who drove my life. Mama could have been living vicariously through me. She was a soprano and studied at the Teachers' College. She taught piano and voice and became a church musician. Mama directed the church's children's choir and the adult choir. Long before I served as an accompanist for university, community, and church choirs directed by brilliant directors and clinicians and directors like my friend Dirk Donahue, I played for

Mama's choirs. She was the first choral director I played for. I was eight. She must have felt ecstatic that she passed on the music gene to her eldest daughter. She passed on the gene to all her children, except that I was the only one who became a professional musician. Mama was determined to be my constant companion, chaperone, and coach. But she worked in tandem with Daddy.

Daddy engineered much of my life. He was, after all, the patriarch. Nothing happened in the family without his approval. His words overruled any slight disparity of opinion between Papa and Mama. Daddy, without question, approved my conservatory studies upon being invited by Mrs. Stella Brimo to be her student at St. Paul's College Conservatory of Music. I was progressing well in my studies. While Mama did the scrapbooking to collect and record the memories, Daddy initiated financial arrangements immediately with Uncle Mel to send money for a new piano and for the piano books to be ordered and directly shipped to our house from the publisher's warehouse in New York City. It seemed like a package of music books arrived each week from America: Mozart and Beethoven Sonatas, Mozart and Beethoven Concertos, complete volumes of Chopin works, Bach Inventions and Preludes and Fugues, piano works of Rachmaninoff, Liszt, Grieg, Mendelssohn, Schubert, Schumann, and Debussy. Daddy was building my music library! When I received the acceptance to study in the United States, Daddy followed through the application process and applied for my U.S. visa. He ultimately decided that I should go and continue my musical studies in New

York City. In reality, who do you think has stage-mom syndrome? I left most of those books behind when I left for New York in 1972. But the same Uncle Mel paid for the new books I now needed in America. In 1990, Mama finally moved to Canada with my sister, Loida, and my brother, Gedeon, to join sister Noemi and her family. Mama brought along in huge boxes a portion of that library. That was her present for me after having been separated for 18 years.

Not the Nervous Kind

Because of the regularity of having to navigate the complex social dynamics of influential circles and performing on the spot for family, friends, and guests, I learned to conquer my nerves at a very early age. You might say I had a lot of practice in managing stage fright, a pesky adversary detrimental to any performer's success. I will say, though, with all the family support surrounding me, that when it came down to my performances, I was all alone to fend for myself—alone to bask in the glory of success and deal with misfortune. But I will add that having been thrown into the fire of competition and the public arena was in itself a valuable private lesson about life. So, I forged ahead.

After the initial failure in the radio-singing contest, I won my first TV talent contest when I was six years old at *Tawag Ng Tanghalan* (translated as "a call to exhibit or to perform"). This "live" talent show has been a Filipino entertainment staple since 1953 at the ABS-CBN television station. It has morphed over the years into what it is today: an exclusive amateur singing competition. I played *Le Secret* on the piano, an intermediate-level piece with lots of staccato and oozing with cuteness. I wore a yellow traditional Filipino attire with butterfly sleeves. I was undaunted. The performance exuded confidence and joy. It helped that my teacher picked an age-appropriate piece that showcased my developing technique and extroverted performance side. The extended family, church folks, the neighbors, and everyone that my parents and grandparents contacted tuned in the television that night. A star was born.

The first major piano competition I won was the Philippine Young Artist Competition at age eleven. The contest introduced me to the stiff and scrutinizing evaluation by adjudicators and critics in the Manila arts circle. I also had the opportunity to win top honors in my age category and perform with the Manila Symphony Orchestra.

Nerves have never been a problem for me. Like I said, I was probably too young to even realize what being nervous meant. I have been blessed with a family who appropriately affirmed me growing up. "Appropriately" is accurate because, in retrospect, the positive reinforcement I received was never too much or too little. My being talented meant only that I had to practice more. It was a matter of stewardship, according to my family. They were considerate of my feelings and worked hard to ensure that the fame and success didn't go to my head. However, I was the one who ultimately let it affect me. I experienced a lack of confidence, which was unusual for me. Yet, I still wondered about the signs of nervousness I had shown in my younger years. Being nervous meant just a slight fluttering in my stomach, but nothing too serious beyond that would harm my concentration. Being nervous elicited a yawning ritual before every performance. Did I need to take a nap? No. The yawning was stress-induced, and it happened backstage a lot. Being nervous meant I got cold fingers, but never clammy hands, before a performance. Once the concert got started, I would quickly settle down, and the ten warm fingers would get to work like little soldiers carrying out their marching orders. No need to wear warming gloves. I did not experience profuse sweating of the palms. No need to carry a handkerchief to ritualistically wipe my hands or the piano keys.

Nervous or not, confident or not, I would still introspect around concert time, sometimes ambivalent about my fleeting childhood. I became an adult too soon. I was cognizant of the fact that I tried to compose myself like one. But a combination of an overprotective and strict upbringing and a deliberate design to shield me from the real world, but thrust into the typical family drama and dysfunction, bred a feeling of isolation in my younger idealistic self. Deep down, I longed just to be a normal kid without all the hoopla. I longed for some downtime. I longed to hang out more freely and longer with friends. I longed to be rid of this persona of snobbish, better-than-any-kid-in-town. I longed to fill my hours with so much wonder for the possibilities of what I could have been spending my time on instead of practicing. How I wish I had been more intentional about journaling to have saved more memories. But even a simple hobby like that would have been viewed by Daddy as a waste of precious time.

"Dear Diary" messages were only for the lazy daydreaming type, he would say. That I was an introspective child was woefully overlooked, a quality not quite understood by my pragmatic grandfather.

I was mature for my age, but my younger self had been through a gamut of life experiences that were but preparation for the many challenges that were about to come my way: Leaving the Philippines at sixteen, learning to assimilate into American culture, and navigating the competitive world of classic art music. I had to navigate married life, being a mother, balancing family and career, engaging in church ministry leadership, attending graduate school while raising two little girls with my husband, and completing a doctoral program. I had been training all along for a life that, for all the mountains of success, victories, good health, and joy of family and friends, also involved deep valleys of loneliness, excruciating mental and emotional pain, and even self-doubt. Life is hard and complicated. Sometimes, finding respite from it all is elusive. The nagging questions pile up. Do I keep going? Do I give up? No matter what, will I be able to take it to the end?

My First Piano Teachers

Miss Imelda Duran was my first piano teacher when I turned five. The story goes that I asked Mama for piano lessons. Although Mama could have taught me piano, Mama believed that the best way to maintain discipline and commitment was to secure an outside teacher for me. She asked for her friends' advice. One of them recommended

Miss Duran who happened to already be teaching private students in a nearby community. Miss Duran was a student of Stella Goldenberg Brimo, a prominent music pedagogue in Manila. Miss Duran was pursuing her piano degree at Santa Isabel College. She came to the house to give lessons.

When Noemi turned five, she also began taking lessons. Pretty soon, both my sisters were taking lessons, then my cousins across the street followed suit. Miss Duran quickly blocked off much of Saturday to teach in our neighborhood. I remember she arranged a big recital for all her students at her college auditorium, from beginners to advanced level, maybe 25 to 30 of us. It was Noemi's first performance. With her winsome bravura, she performed a simple beginning-level piece. She was outstanding and stole the show. I played *Malagueña* by Ernesto Lecuona. I could hardly reach the pedals but managed to steady myself with my right foot on the sustain pedal as I balanced the rest of me at the edge of the piano seat. A few weeks after our event, Miss Duran performed her senior recital, a partial requirement of her bachelor of music degree. Her repertoire included the performance of the first movement of the *Brahms Piano Concerto #2 in Bb Major,* which according to Miss Duran, happened to be her teacher's signature concerto, one her pedagogue had performed several times with an orchestra. Miss Duran secured a piano accompanist for her recital. Many of her students attended the concert with their parents. That was when I first caught a glimpse of her piano teacher, a tall distinguished-looking woman, blond, fair, silky-skinned, and blue-eyed. The lady registered charisma all over the room, yet dutifully doted on her graduating student.

There was no doubt Miss Duran set up my music foundational skills. She did not only teach me proper technique and expression, but also solfège and conducting. I was able to comfortably conduct multiple directing patterns at the age of eight while singing the given melody in solfège. She hammered down the scales and arpeggios unapologetically. She demanded consistent

I had been training all along for a life that, for all the mountains of success, victories, good health, and joy of family and friends, also involved deep valleys of loneliness, excruciating mental and emotional pain, and even self-doubt.

practice and lesson preparedness. What a unique conservatory-like experience in a private lesson! The last recital I played under Miss Duran's tutelage was two years later. I performed the first movement of a Mozart concerto. She accompanied me on a second piano. It was the final number of her annual student recital.

The road to Juilliard began when I met Stella Brimo. Miss Duran invited her to hear me play at that recital. I did not know at the time that Miss Duran had already discussed with my parents the possibility of asking her teacher to take me on as a student. I was finally introduced to Mrs. Brimo after the recital. She was sophisticated and reserved but cordial. I recall her having a serious conversation with my parents and Daddy by the grand piano. Of course, I was not part of it. Before I knew it, I was enrolled at the St. Paul's College Conservatory of Music after the summer break to study under her. The change in music teachers proved pivotal in my music career. She was a concert pianist who became more famous for developing young talented pianists. Wow! It was an honor; it was intimidating, but I was hungry for the next level. I was only ten.

The Brimos were upper-class folks who lived in one of the most exclusive neighborhoods in Greater Manila. Stella Goldenberg Brimo was of French Jewish descent. She was a socialite, part of the city's elite cultural community. Her husband, Dr. John G. Brimo, was a rather quiet gentleman. I had the privilege of taking lessons at their home. Upon entering the house on my first lesson, her assistant led Mama and me upstairs into her teaching studio at the end of a long hallway. The large room featured one entire wall decked with shelves upon shelves of bound music books, color-coded and alphabetized according to the composer's name. Bach was brown, Beethoven was navy blue, Chopin was red, Debussy was yellow-green, Mozart in maroon, Mendelssohn in forest green, and Rachmaninoff was aqua blue. There was even fuchsia, though I can't remember now which composer was fuchsia. It was impressive! I came home from that first lesson talking up a storm about Mrs. Brimo's teaching studio. I was enthralled by the sheer volume and visual palette of my teacher's collection, a reaction similar to Belle's admiration of the Beast's massive library. I told Daddy that I'd never seen anything like it. Wouldn't you know that Mrs. Brimo's music library became the inspiration for the kind of music library Daddy dreamed of for me? As soon as my music books arrived from New York City, Daddy also had the books professionally bound and color-coded to each composer, just like Mrs. Brimo's. The smaller collection became a miniature replica of Mrs. Brimo's.

The Brimo Manor peeked behind tall cement walls. The garden area was beautifully landscaped with mature trees and foliage, evoking the exotic lushness of a rainforest. I remember my first dinner party at her house. The tables, which were impeccably decorated with more knives, forks, and teaspoons than one person could ever use during one meal, flowed from the dining area to the back patio garden. I was mesmerized by the sophisticated tone of the evening. Elegant tablecloths and napkins, meticulously arranged fresh flowers grazed each table, the soft dinging of crystal glasses, and the aroma of a fine dining menu was a feast for the senses. Fortunately, I already completed my table manners training. I successfully demonstrated my social skills at my first of several sit-down dinners at my teacher's house, as though I was the product of some fancy boarding school. I was only eleven years old, mature and composed, but young and naïve.

I received a full scholarship to study with Mrs. Brimo. She offered to teach me for free. Could I get any luckier? I hit the jackpot for sure! Like the old TV game show *Let's Make A Deal*, Mrs. Brimo showed me doors and doors of surprises to select except, unlike the game show, Mrs. Brimo never had a bad door. Each door led me to an opportunity and a blessing. Under her tutelage, I took the scales and arpeggios to new heights. I learned pieces from a variety of period styles and composers. The way she taught Mozart, highlighting her conscientious approach to achieving the right touch and ethos of colliding child-like innocence and brilliance, was, I think, the most enjoyable way to study Mozart. I played in master classes and entered several competitions.

The Brimos later moved to a larger residence in another exclusive part of town but farther away. Her new teaching studio was even more spacious. The grand piano sat close to the center of the room with an upright to one side to facilitate a piano concerto session with your accompanist. The location of the Brimo residence meant that our commute by public transportation would be longer. We had to switch from a bus to two jeepneys, then a cab, the only way to reach our final destination if you were not driving a car. It seemed like forever to get to a lesson.

Mrs. Brimo was affectionate to her students. In all her sophisticated aura, she was the same sweet mentor to all of us of various ages and stages of development. You know the customary practice of giving your piano teacher a small gift for Christmas? Try the opposite. She gave each of her piano students a Christmas present. Not just any Christmas present either, but one that came with sweet sentiments. She was a thoughtful teacher who showered me with gifts for my birthday, Christmas, and special performance occasions. Jewelry was a favorite of hers. My favorite was a gold bracelet with my name engraved on it with the date of my premiere recital. I still have that bracelet. I also remember my first Christmas gift from Mrs. Brimo. It was a beautiful doll, about 16 inches, encased in an even more luxurious box. I did not know what to do with it. A sad commentary on my life was that I really did not know how to play with dolls. The doll was so pretty and probably quite expensive. So I just stared at the doll with a mixed feeling of awe and panic. The gift stayed intact in its exquisite box, and I forgot about it until now. So what was that all about? What did I miss? A child who did not appreciate a toy doll—an awareness that dawned on me with much sadness.

Mrs. Brimo and her husband were devoted patrons of the arts. They held subscriptions to the most sought-after concerts at the most prestigious venues in Manila. This kind of lifestyle was beyond logic among us simple city folks. Such lavish spending on cultural events did not align with our stringent entertainment budget, limited to listening to "live" radio talent shows. Who would pay an exorbitant price for a concert ticket, endure the hassle of dressing up, and catch two to three jeepneys just to reach the concert hall? Then, you'd have to listen to an unfamiliar performer for more than two and a half hours surrounded by people who seem out of your league—dressed and behaving like superstars on the Academy Awards red carpet. Afterward, you'd face the same transportation challenge to get back home at midnight. Not me!

However, my chaperone mom and I easily became the benefactors of the Brimos' subscription and generosity. Mrs.

Brimo handed us free tickets after free tickets—a concert almost every other week. Our grateful attitude was only eclipsed by our concern about keeping up with the peripheral expenses that came with the indulgence of a high-cultured diet: The concert attire, the travel cost, the pre-concert or post-concert dining, and souvenirs. But to have witnessed a live performance by the Russian Bolshoi ballet troupe from the third-row orchestra section when I was only eleven was beyond words. It was like being transported to another world. I sat motionless and mesmerized by the magnificence and perfect synchronization of movement, music, and staging. I questioned my choice of artistic endeavor. I should have been a ballerina! I had the incredible opportunity to watch international artists and world-renowned pianists, such as Vladimir Ashkenazy and Ann Schein. It made me wonder what planet I was living on! Free, world-class entertainment does not happen to everyone.

A Few More Gigs

Mrs. Brimo introduced me to Oscar Yatco, a concert violinist and the dashing, young, dynamic conductor of the Manila Symphony Orchestra. I performed under his baton several times, one of which was most memorable. Under Brimo's tutelage, I played for her—First Lady Imelda Marcos at Luneta's open-air auditorium at Jose Rizal Park. I had just performed my premiere recital months earlier. Mrs. Marcos was the primary sponsor of the music event, part of a park concert series. The program featured two child prodigies. First, I performed the first movement of the Mendelssohn

Piano Concerto in G minor. Then, a young up-and-coming 13-year-old boy played the first movement of the well-known Mendelssohn *Violin Concerto in E minor.* We both delivered dynamic and riveting performances, each even more outstanding than usual, considering our young ages and predisposition to brilliant fast tempi. Two orchestral members, the principal flutist and the principal clarinetist, dubbed us the Mendelssohn double threat. The principal flutist incessantly teased us into becoming a teenage romantic couple. We would eventually be paired up again to perform at another concert event. By the second concert, the flutist and clarinetist called our duo pairing the "Mendelssohn sweethearts." I was annoyed. But what did I know? I was only twelve years old.

I remember practicing how to curtsy days and weeks before the concert. That's how you greet the Madame, according to Mama. Mama insisted that I get it right, which foot to go behind the other, the proper knee bend, the upright body position, and with that slight head bow. I wore an off-white, short-length dress with a heavily beaded and sequined bodice. It was comparable to an evening cocktail dress but appropriate for a twelve-year-old. How a young girl was expected to perform in a dress with a torso that felt more like a straight jacket was beyond me. But I looked gorgeous, nonetheless.

I met Madame after the performance. I had only read about her in the newspapers and magazines. She was a gorgeous woman, perfectly put together, 5'7", tall for a Filipino woman. She was, of course, wearing a floor-length evening gown with her signature butterfly sleeves. I curtsied correctly. She made some perfunctory remarks about how fantastic my performance was. What I remember the most was that she looked me in the eye and gave me an approving nod and smile. The Madame was pleased. That was enough for me.

I was invited to play again with the Manila Symphony at a special concert at Camp Aguinaldo, the headquarters of the armed forces of the Philippines. Shortly after, we headed to the mountains, north of Manila. An identical concert was performed in Baguio's military base, Camp Henry T. Allen, complete with a radio station interview. I remember the large crowd gathered outside. I was whisked to a microphone to answer a question in the open air. I did not understand all the fuss about a prepubescent child. It's not like I'm a pop idol. I was a serious child so I must not have been a fun guest, unlike the brilliant extroverted children who grace the Ellen DeGeneres and Steve Harvey shows. But I recall how much I enjoyed the attention. We went inside for the sit-down interview. It was a lifetime ago.

I remember the first time the word *pinch hitter* was used to describe what I was about to do. I knew there was the so-called pinch hitter in baseball, the substitute, called to bat for the pitcher or any other player. I was called to pinch hit for a well-known concert pianist and pedagogue when I was fourteen. I had never been asked to do anything last minute, with only a two-day notice, much less be invited to take the place of a rock star pianist. Benjamin Tupas was one of a small group of elite Filipino piano virtuosos of his generation. He was known for having produced and sent abroad talented pianists who won international piano competitions that launched their careers. Mr. Tupas was to play the Gershwin *Rhapsody in Blue* for a gala performance for the United States of America Ambassador to the Republic of the Philippines, Henry A. Byroade. Mr. Tupas became ill. Mama got a call from my teacher. I had just performed the Gershwin piece with the orchestra a few months earlier. Mrs. Brimo deemed I was ready to pinch hit. A rehearsal had already been scheduled for Mr. Tupas; I just had to step in. We rehearsed the following day. We performed the next evening. It seemed like child's play to me back then. No pressure; it just felt good I got to perform again. I think I did not mind rubbing elbows with the who's who of Manila's high society and American diplomats.

I performed a few live TV shows, thanks to Papa's connections at the network station. I would like to think that I was asked to appear in these shows because the directors and producers simply liked him. The performances were simple, usually limited to a short piano piece for each show. On one occasion, I was given an impromptu direction to "act" but play myself in a skit of a live variety show, similar to the Ed Sullivan show. Come to think of it, I can't believe I was once a TV child actor who delivered improvised lines.

The gigs kept coming. When Papa announced that the producer of *An Evening with Pilita* invited me to the show, I was stunned. I thought I hit the big time. *An Evening with Pilita* was a pre-taped one-hour musical show that aired once a week featuring Pilita Corrales. Ms. Corrales is a Filipino pop singer, songwriter, actress, and comedian all in one. I loved her movies, and I loved her show. I was to be her "classical" musical guest for one entire month. My assignment was to play one piano piece a week. I had not done any prior recording. Every performance had been in front of a live audience. There was no audience for the taping, just a grand piano against a background set and the TV crew. I recorded a piece per show for five consecutive weeks. The process was tedious. The taping sessions tried the patience of a twelve-year-old, already distracted by an unfamiliar performance environment. I relished on performing to a live audience, so the absence of one was the antithesis to any performance. First, an audio recording had to be made. That took about four to five takes until I was satisfied with the result. After the audio recording, I was then going to be filmed, again playing, but now trying to be in sync with the selected recorded performance.

It took four takes to get the visual to what the director thought was show-ready. Take three or take four was not what I wanted to hear. I had an impatient predisposition that held steadfastly to the notion that if something was not good enough the first time around, what was the point of all that practicing if you could not shine on that one given moment? The first two tapings turned out to be disastrous because all the lighting and production gear in the studio proved to be incredibly distracting. What a laborious experience! Compounding the recording and filming time was the number of times I had to stop for one reason or another. The recording and filming process of a four-minute piece amounted to five hours! Why couldn't they have shot a video? Oh, I forgot, this was back in 1969.

The road to Juilliard was constructed by the combination of unique experiences and opportunities that came my way and the deliberate attention of my family and piano teachers to build the necessary steps to cultivate my piano skills so people would notice. Performing local concerts and making TV appearances gave me confidence to overcome stage fright. The dedication of my early piano teachers for me to achieve steady progress in technique and musicianship was a hallmark of my strong music foundation. Playing in the presence of the first lady of the country and the last-minute serendipitous substitution to perform for an indisposed concert pianist became newsworthy. Call it luck. Call it a blessing. I was grateful for the destination.

5 | GROWING UP FILIPINO

I am Filipino by birth, and Filipinos fluctuate, between calling ourselves Asian and Pacific Islander, depending on the presence or absence of the Pacific Islanders category on any given survey. But for the sake of simplicity, I will say that growing up Asian and a child prodigy almost sounds redundant. The stereotype of Asian children excelling in sciences, math, or the arts is perpetuated by images of strict, stoic-looking Asian parents urging their children to succeed in these areas. However, is it a stereotype or more like the norm? I should know. I was born into a home where parents, grandparents, uncles, and aunts might have a say in the discipline of the younger generation. Anyone can offer their opinion, well-meaning or not, about the children's schooling with expectations to excel and get high grades. Having lived in New York and New Jersey, I have taught children of Filipino, Japanese, Chinese, Korean, Taiwanese, and Indonesian immigrants. I observed among the families an air of strict and authoritarian decorum. I should know! As hard as I tried not to be the typical Asian mom, I am well aware that my two now-grown daughters, born in the United States, did not escape a form of Asian upbringing. They heard it in my tone of voice and my Filipino accent. They managed to traverse Dad and Mom's strict and unreasonable rules of curfew and dating. High academic expectation was typical.

To be the best among the best is what is acceptable and respectable in the culture. Overachieving is highly esteemed. Studying, reading, and long hours of doing homework are the norm. Playing an instrument is encouraged. Playing sports and participating in extracurricular activities when I was growing up typically had no place in an Asian home, especially not in the Philippines or any other country on the other side of the Western hemisphere. Of course, it's a different world today. The more extracurricular activities in your background, the better the chances of landing a spot and a scholarship at the higher ranked schools. In addition to team sports, add gymnastics, swimming, student government, community volunteering, another musical instrument, and the list goes on. However, in the family I inherited, we often heard the argument: why would you waste your time playing with a ball when you can study diligently for a chance to get ahead in life? I believed the word "fun" did not exist in our family vocabulary.

Achieving something through hard work is a source of ethnic pride among Asians. It brings honor to the family. It serves as a model for success. It is a way of life. So discipline, as in the formal study of music, starts early, as soon as the child's chin can hold up a violin or a three-year-old can climb on top of a piano bench. The search for a child prodigy is always a hopeful possibility!

One of the most successful and enduring contemporary Asian artists of Chinese descent is Yo-Yo Ma, a child prodigy on the cello at five years old. Ma attended Juilliard and later Harvard. Sarah Chang, of Korean descent, is an internationally acclaimed violinist. Chang began attending Juilliard at age five. Lang Lang, a Chinese child prodigy, has become the 21st century's classical piano rock star because of YouTube and the Beijing Olympics. Lang Lang started his lessons at the age of three and performed his first public concert when he was five. By the time he began his studies at age fifteen at Philadelphia's Curtis Institute of Music, Lang Lang had already won piano competitions and concertized in China, Germany, and Japan. These artists represent the crème de la crème. Their biographical journeys are captivating, each unique but encapsulating the experiences, enigma, and essence of a child prodigy. But there are thousands upon thousands of others, perhaps not at the level of world renown, whose stories have not been heard, a story like mine.

I began piano lessons when I was five years old at the same time I started kindergarten. That was the typical age to begin musical studies. As I said, it was my brilliant idea to learn to play the instrument.

By the time I was age three, Mama and a *yaya* (a Filipino nanny, which is quite different from the glamorous image of nannies in wealthy families) had already taught me to read and write the English alphabet. By age four, I was reading children's books in English. I learned addition and subtraction before kindergarten. I was a confident but rather subdued child. If I had any precocious tendencies on the piano, I believe either my family did not recognize it right away, or perhaps I kept it to myself. But I vividly remember my very first piano lesson. I had an epiphany moment during the lesson. Playing the piano was going to be a blast. It seemed easy and enjoyable. Even as a child, I thought I could make a career out of it. But where did this come from? The debate on nature versus nurture will tilt towards one side when you examine my pedigree. I am certain that my musical heritage and legacy did not start with me.

Mama was the eldest of four children. She was fourteen by the time the sweeping arm of World War II reached the Philippines after the bombing of Pearl Harbor. Her family survived the Japanese invasion and lived through the liberation of the Philippines by the Americans led by General Douglas MacArthur. I knew this part of history because family members told the story repeatedly over the years. After the war was over, Mama went to school to become a teacher. She studied voice and piano. One can almost trace my predisposition to music studies to my mother's background. Mama became a voice and piano teacher. She was also the church choir director.

Papa played the guitar. He leaned towards classical guitar, although he also played Filipino pop ballads. My siblings and I heard the story of how Papa and Mama met, one that was loaded with clichés reminiscent of a typical corny Filipino B-rated movie. Mama and her family were living in a post-war new development just outside Manila. Papa's younger sister and her new husband also began building a modest house in the same development directly across the street from Daddy's home. Papa became the night watch during the construction. To pass the long evening hours, Uncle Mel related that Papa would play his guitar and sing *kundiman,* traditional Filipino love songs. Mama heard the crooning from across the street and later found out the name of the gentleman who was rendering beautiful melodies in the evening. We like to think that Papa serenaded Mama, what we call *harana* in Tagalog. We thought that such stories were only in the movies, but music, indeed, brought them together.

Although the guitar and the *banduria* were popular in the Philippines, the favored instrument in our family was the piano. Almost everyone in my family played the piano. Mama was classically trained. Her siblings, Uncle Lerry, Auntie Nora, and Uncle Mel, could all play the piano by ear very well and were able to accompany the group's singing and hum

> Achieving something through hard work is a source of ethnic pride among Asians. It brings honor to the family.

a tune while playing. My father's baby sister, Auntie Encar, was only ten years older than me and she also played the piano. She was the one who showed me how to play hymns the fancy way, with all the decorative notes and octaves, to accompany congregational singing. She eventually became a missionary and married a Thai minister and Bible translator. They settled in Bangkok. Noemi, Loida, and Gedeon also play the piano, and so do several of my cousins on my father's side. The musical tendencies were inescapable in my extended family. It was a way of life for us. I've always heard it said that Filipinos are musical by nature. I tend to agree that the musical influence in our culture runs deep.

It's been said that Filipinos are great singers. The Philippines produced a few successful international stars. I think the most popular of them are Lea Salonga and Arnel Pineda of the band Journey. Music is deeply rooted in Filipino culture. Our family's favorite pastime was gathering around the piano and singing. This occurred regularly at my childhood home. It was how we spent time together and entertained ourselves. The repertoire spanned the gamut of eclectic selections, from a wide range of beloved traditional Tagalog ballads like *Dahil Sa Iyo* (Because of You) to the Filipino folk songs *Bahay Kubo* (My Humble Hut) and *Paruparung Bukid* (Butterfly in the Field), from the melodic tender serenades during courtship to the popular songs of the day, whether English Billboard top 100 songs or pop hits in Tagalog. Mama would perform her repertoire of sacred vocal literature and a few arias from operas. For a time, we included *Cursilista* songs in the list. The songs were sung in Bible study groups in Catholic homes. The emotional rendition of gospel hymns ("How Great Thou Art" was a favorite) in Protestant homes and churches was also a significant part of the Filipino singing landscape. The pianists and piano players in the family took turns in accompanying the soloists or group singing. When the hymns were sung towards the end of the sing-along evening, an extended prayer time would follow.

Although it was so easy to feign classical snobbery because of my training, I slowly began to develop an appreciation for a variety of music styles and genres as I experienced the meaningful family music gatherings. My family's mixed bag of musical background convinced me that I did not have to be boxed into any one style. It is no wonder I've embraced music beyond Chopin. Who would have thought that the snooty conservatory kid would eventually listen and enjoy a few jazz genres, Broadway musicals, bluegrass, rhythm and blues, a cappella (where are the instruments?), and Gaither Vocal Band? Today, the singing tradition in Asian homes continues with the emergence of karaoke in the 1980s.

Pampered, Privileged, Protected

I was a spoiled brat. Growing up in the Philippines with a *yaya* and a maid, I enjoyed the trappings of a privileged life by Filipino standards. We were not, by any means, crazy-rich Asians, but we were comfortable because we had uncles who lived abroad and supported the family back home. So I never had to make my bed, clean my room, do laundry, cook, wash the dishes, or clean the house. I had no idea what chores were. All I had to do was sleep, eat, study well, practice the piano, go to church, play for church, and simply be this overbearing, pampered, bratty, demanding, bossy oldest sister/cousin to everyone. No problem. I did that so well!

I heard it said enough, day in and day out, that my hands were valuable and irreplaceable—that washing dishes by hand, since we did not own a dishwasher, would only ruin my precious little fingers. A few well-intentioned relatives argued that my fingers should have probably been insured anyway because they were potentially the means to earn a living and to a better life. Although I was excused from household chores, I missed out on many simple experiences that normal children enjoy, such as playing carefree in the streets, climbing trees, and riding bicycles—activities that could be considered risky for my hands.

The main family house, Daddy's house, had four second-floor bedrooms, one on each corner of the house. Each bedroom door opened into a huge central common area, much like a bonus room today. The common area was large enough that beds were posted, one on each opposite end of the room, for guests like cousins and second cousins. We still had plenty of space for a gathering room upstairs. When Daddy built the house in the early 1950s in a flood-prone zone (well, all the islands are flood-prone), he had the foresight to create a space upstairs to hold his big family when typhoons arrived in the monsoon seasons.

A fond memory during a typhoon was that while the grown-ups enjoyed the comforts of the bedrooms and extra beds, all the grandchildren had more fun sleeping across the center room on bamboo mats, much like a pajama party. While the howling wind and torrential buckets of rain pounded on the wooden window shutters, while the waters covered an inch or two of the ground floor, children upstairs feasted on typhoon food of rice, diced fresh tomatoes, and *bagoóng alamáng* (fermented shrimp condiment) or rice with *tuyô* (dried fish) and Spam. We also spooked one another in the dark with ghost stories.

We had three areas of dining. The first one, right next to the living room, was the formal dining room, where we only ate when we had guests over. That's when the fine china would come out of hiding. A china cabinet complemented the formal table. Right behind the dining room, through a small open arch, was the second eating room area with a big circular table that would allow for a Chinese-style dinner. The refrigerator was located in this room, filled with cold, bottled chocolate milk, bottled soda, and fresh goat cheese. A door right next to the table opened to the dreaded storeroom. It functioned like a pantry where lidded barrels of rice and other staples were kept. This room was also a haven for creeping, disgusting insect creatures. What did we expect? We were on a tropical island. There was a large sink with two huge barrel drums containing water for daily use. A more casual atmosphere permeated this space. I remember that Sunday after-church dinners were served in this room. I couldn't wait for Sundays because chicken most likely would be on the menu. We only ate chicken on Sundays whenever Lola decided which one of her chickens running in the backyard was ready to be served.

But I think the best part of the house was the back kitchen, beyond the round table room. This was where the real cooking and dining happened. It's what I think of when I think of home. I could almost savor the familiar aroma of a home-cooked meal, comfort food at its best. I could picture the chaotic scrambling of flip-flops and bare feet as grandchildren hurriedly took their seats because Daddy was about to say grace for lunch. The back kitchen contained a large old-fashioned firewood stove made of stone and cement. It came in handy during typhoon season when we lost electricity. A small portable gas range with a small oven also stood next to it. It was the best of both worlds of culinary cooking. The family gathered around a long, wooden, rectangular picnic-like table and benches. The daily fare we could expect was mostly rice, fish, and vegetables. The menu was dictated by Daddy's preferred healthier diet. Once a week or so, Mama would make Western-influenced foods like spaghetti or hamburgers. The extended family ate together here in shifts. What I remember was that grandparents and children ate first, then the rest of the grown-ups, whoever was around.

A huge kitchen sink completed the back kitchen structure. There always seemed to be running water when you turned on the kitchen faucet, but it was only an illusion because the water came from a huge outside cement vat that collected water during specific hours when the government opened the lines for residents to collect water. This explains the barrel drums in the second dining room, if you were wondering. I loved the kitchen sink because it did appear like we had running water, and how cool was that! I remember I would volunteer to help wash the dishes. I enjoyed the sensation of soapy water running down my little hands through the plates and utensils. It was like a timeout for me—a timeout from the grind of my scheduled practicing. To be able to wash dishes and, in the process, play at the sink, was not an obligatory chore for me at all. I loved it.

Outside of the home-cooked meals at the house, Mama, mindful of the kind of rigorous schedule I kept, did not fail to treat me to something special after Saturday conservatory classes. One of the places Mama would take me was to the Emporium in downtown Manila, a one-building mall several stories high. After several music classes, I would be starving by mid-afternoon, ready to devour anything for a late lunch. I enjoyed ordering a Filipino hamburger with ketchup and Coca-Cola at one of the eateries. The weekly dining ritual was the unspoken reward for a day's work at the conservatory. I thought the Emporium hamburger was the best burger ever. When I moved to New York a few years later, I found out what a real burger was supposed to look and taste like. I had my first McDonald's hamburger in 1972. What I had been eating all those years in Manila was more of a Filipino version of a meatloaf sandwich. I felt duped. Another place to dine and unwind was a sandwich shop within blocks of the conservatory. Not having learned the word "gourmet" yet in 1969, I would describe the food as high-priced sandwiches and ice cream sundaes. The eatery was an upper-class establishment. I felt like we did not belong there, although I loved the fancy food anyway.

Another culinary destination was the Quiapo district, where numerous small stores amalgamated into a huge semi-indoor marketplace. Eating during the mid-afternoon was called a *merienda*, the Filipino tradition of grabbing a small bite to tide us over until supper. The so-called snack time could either be sweet or savory. Our favorite places included a black bean *hopia* shop to satisfy our sweet tooth.

The delicacies were made fresh for the day. Another option was *halo-halo*, a mixture of a little bit of everything: sweet beans, sweet garbanzos, *leche flan* (baked custard), *ube* (purple yam delicacy), baby coconut preserves, sweet corn, sweet bananas, and other ingredients all mixed (*halo-halo* means "mixed-mixed") in a tall glass with crushed ice and evaporated milk. It is a refreshing Filipino treat. One other must-stop was a small hole-in-the-wall where you could find *lugaw* or *congee*, a hot rice porridge with a garnish of sliced boiled eggs, fried garlic pieces, and chopped green onions. It's comfort food all right.

Not wanting to be left out of the reward system he and Mama set up, Daddy motivated me with edible fruits and chocolates. Grapes and apples were luxury items but occasionally appeared in the house as an incentive to practice more. Daddy would also buy Baby Ruth chocolate bars, although I did not care for them. Maybe he thought that rewarding me with a chocolate bar with my namesake would be more special. But I had no idea who Babe Ruth or The Bambino was, and I couldn't care less anyway, if indeed, the candy bar was named after him. What I loved was the large-sized Cadbury Fruit and Nut bar after a good piano lesson. Yes, I worked hard. I played hard. Needless to say, I also ate very well because I was pampered, protected, and a princess.

When I thought I'd been spoiled rotten to the hilt, voilà, another surprise! Mrs. Brimo, in another of her best efforts to assist the family's need for transportation, arranged for her chauffeur to pick me up after school to get me to my weekday piano lesson. Could I feel any more protected? Mama and I were relieved of the multiple public transportation transfers and connections, instead, now safely cocooned in an air-conditioned vehicle. I got an early dismissal approval. Of course, I felt like a celebrity. Nobody else got early dismissal privileges. A Cadillac with a chauffeur, parked outside the front main entrance of the school, whisked me away to my piano lesson each week. Mama would already be in the car.

A few of my school friends, whom I would consider rich, had chauffeurs drive them to school. Mama and I were public transportation-dependent. Rich people lived behind high concrete walls or gated communities in modern architecture mansions in exclusive neighborhoods. We lived in a modest semi-compound, with small cottage-sized homes surrounding the main house. Rich people had washing machines, air conditioning, and a maid for every category of chores. We had a maid who washed our clothes and linens by hand on the back patio. Our address, though miles away from the more notorious gang neighborhoods, still suggested the presence of *kanto* boys (young men), dawdling at street corners, gawking at young girls, and inviting trouble. Rich people lived along boulevards with "no loitering" signs. Rich people sent their children to Catholic all-girl schools or all-boy schools with room and board. They were guaranteed some of the best education on the islands from members of religious orders such as The Missionary Sisters of the Immaculate Conception, the Society of Jesus, the Dominican Order, or the Order of Saint Benedict. I attended Immaculate Conception Academy of Manila; not in a prestigious zip code, it was a commuter school with no dormitories with a clientele of middle-class children whose parents were teachers, small business owners, civil service workers, doctors, nurses, engineers, and homemakers. Nevertheless, this middle-class kid quickly developed a taste for the finer things in life. The classical music world with all its sophisticated trappings, as might be expected, fostered a pampered lifestyle.

So Far So Good Until . . .

Though a prodigious existence was carefully and strictly monitored in terms of time management and a rigid schedule, it was a life with purpose and expected good outcomes. It was the kind of living I had always known. It's my normal, and I could handle that. So far so good—until I got very sick.

Towards the end of seventh grade, I came down with an unknown illness and was hospitalized for two weeks. From my recollection, the doctors back then thought that it might have been meningitis. I remember being placed flat on my stomach while the doctor extracted fluid from my spine. It turned out not to be meningitis, but it was not specifically anything else, either. I battled a high fever. The final diagnosis was that I contracted a kind of viral infection. I guess viral infection was the default diagnosis when an illness could not be explained back in the day. It took another two months of recovery at home. I was obviously out of school the whole time. I was supposed to have graduated in late March from seventh grade.

In the '60s, Immaculate Conception Academy of Manila's

education system and similar private schools commenced with Kindergarten, followed by Primary Education (Grades 1-7), and then Secondary Education (four years of high school). There was no middle school back then, although the curriculum beginning in 4th grade became very intensive and progressively more difficult. The K-12 system was adopted in 2012 to reflect Junior High School (Grades 7-10) and Senior High School (Grades 11-12). Getting sick was not an option if you wanted to graduate on time. Because of the hospitalization and subsequent recuperation at home, I had to catch up with schoolwork to be able to take all the required examinations to graduate with my class. I had anticipated finishing at the top of my class. Achieving the highest grade point average and class ranking on graduation day determined whether I would receive a full scholarship in high school. The student who came second would receive a half scholarship. For the first time in my life, I worried about failing and dying.

Catching up with missed lessons and lectures from the uncomfortable position and restriction of your bed, much less studying to pass the exams, was not the way to better health and recovery. It was a close-to-impossible situation! However, I studied and studied. With Mama's help, I tackled question after question, math problem after math problem, and memorized historical and scientific facts. I wrote practice essays on just about any topic Mama would give me. One other thing for sure—I put the idea of practicing piano out of my mind. I was relieved about that. When all was said and done, I graduated valedictorian of the class by a margin of less than a tenth of a point. I received the full scholarship. Luisa, one of my best friends, was a salutatorian. Sadly, I missed the commencement ceremony altogether.

Except for a minor tricycle accident when I was five, I had never been in a hospital that sick. The images of that pivotal life experience are forever etched in my memory. I can still imagine, like the movie in my mind, one strange event in my hospital room following the spinal procedure. I was delirious. The nurses were managing a high fever that would not break. I thought for a moment that I might be hallucinating, but Mama confirmed later, after the fever broke, that I was not.

I was still lying down on my stomach. Mama whispered into my ear that the elders of my evangelical church came to pray over me, along with the oldest female member of our church. They quietly filed into the room, one by one. I did not recognize specific faces as the whole scenario played out hazily and in slow motion. The group surrounded my hospital bed. For about 10-15 minutes, one by one, they took turns uttering prayers I had never heard before—a kind of powerful, exalting, beseeching, wailing plea to the Lord God to heal my body of the undetermined illness. I thought the oldest lady prayed the longest and the most powerful. She was known for it at our church. I would guess one of the elders anointed my head with oil because that was the practice, but I cannot remember. However, what I do recall was the feeling of relief and the confidence that I would recover from this illness. I somehow knew that I would beat this thing.

Then something unexpected that I would consider even more peculiar transpired next, 15 minutes after the church elders left my hospital bed another group of visitors silently entered the room. Even in my delirious state, a lighthearted thought crossed my mind that surely the two groups probably ran into each other downstairs in the lobby or by the hallway. I silently laughed. My saga was beginning to unfold like a scene from a hospital soap opera. A certain sense of an almost out-of-body experience continued to permeate my surroundings.

Mama, in her calm voice sweetly announced, "Ruth, the ICAM sisters are here!" Four nuns from my school appeared in immaculate white habits and black veils, like that of Reverend Mother in *The Sound of Music*. I could see, from the corner of my eye, shoved down on the pillow, the swift-flowing movement of habit hems across the floor. I could hear the soft, rhythmic dangling of the wooden rosary beads hanging from a belt around the sisters' waists. I looked down towards the floor as several pairs of black shoes, plain, sturdy, and laced-up, quietly passed around my bed. I was so captivated by the blurry image and solemn sound that I failed to notice that the sisters had also brought along Father Pelayo, our confessor. I had such a crush on the young priest that, if a nurse were monitoring my vitals, she would have recorded them to have spiked into a slight frenzy the minute I realized who also stepped into my room. The second group of visitors was more subdued and reserved. Their hushed voices were calming in contrast to the palpitating intensity of the prayers of those who preceded them a few minutes earlier. And just like the church elders, the ICAM contingent surrounded my bed and prayed a few Hail Marys and various prayers of supplication. They did not anoint me nor serve me Communion. My soul was comforted. I knew what the last rites were all about. I realized that Father was not administering them that afternoon, so my confidence increased. I began to believe I was not going to meet my Maker that soon. Imagine two devout groups offering strong petitions to God on my behalf, both of which I believe had a direct line to God. So how could I not possibly recover? Church elders on one end, a priest and nuns on the other, I thought I got it all covered. I received a faith booster! But I, too, prayed to God with diligence. I knew that death came very close.

I did not understand then the purpose of the illness; but slowly, as the years unfolded, I discovered that God continued to unravel it, layer by layer, His plans for me according to His will and perfect timing. Since the hospital experience, I continued to see how God has held my hand in the journey of life. I was never the same after that. I discovered a new purpose in my life. Boldness made a grand entrance, the unfamiliar kind that I once thought was uncomfortable. A kind of fearlessness came over me for having closely stared at death. The experience changed my life. I became more determined that no matter what came my way, I would be all right. I would gladly step back into the race of life because God reigns, no matter what!

What I was most thankful for during that difficult time was that when my first year of high school finally began in June, the traumatic hospitalization was behind me. The challenging physical and mental recovery had become a distant memory. Through it all, I was grateful to still have a friend by my side. Even though I edged Luisa by a slim margin to win the full scholarship, she congratulated me right away, and we remained the best of friends for the rest of my ICAM days. Little did I know that the next two years would be my last in the Philippines.

Sometimes a Girl Just Wants to Have Some Fun

The Beatles opened up a new world for the classical snob that I was. I thought that Paul McCartney was cute. I asked myself why I would be the only one left behind playing Bach and Mozart when all my friends were into the British mop tops. So, I followed suit and began consuming the group's fresh sound and the music of Herman's Hermits and The Monkees. I also developed a liking for Simon and Garfunkel (my introduction to folk rock), The Carpenters (the voice and the orchestration), James Taylor (I thought he was the cleanest shaven, guitar-playing hippie since *Fire and Rain* broke out), and, of course, The Jackson 5 (especially the adorable young Michael Jackson) and everyone else coming out of Motown). The snooty musician was learning to be hip. My growing eclectic taste in music took me by surprise. No longer was I confined to the traditional art music of the Baroque, Classical, and Romantic periods or hymns and gospel music of my faith heritage. I discovered a fun kind of Western pop music that was taking the world by storm. To be honest, I couldn't get enough of it.

The rigidity of my schedule occasionally got to me. I was not perfectly compliant. Sometimes, I felt like I needed a break from it all. The rebellious tendency of youth surfaced here and there, fighting for the adventure and simple pleasures of a prepubescent child. I couldn't listen to the Beatles at home for several reasons. First, no pop music was allowed at home, per Daddy's authoritarian rule. It's either classical or church music. Second, the Beatles declared themselves "more popular than Christ" about the same time their plane landed on Philippine soil as part of their Asian concert tour. That announcement did not sit well with Daddy. The Beatles were banned in our household. What could a young girl do to satiate her fancy for the group of good-looking young Brits whose unique style and music propelled their global meteoric rise, the kind that was unheard of during an already restless time in history? I went to my classmates' houses under the pretense of a group project to listen to the latest Beatles' hit. I lied and listened to Beatles' recordings wherever I could.

Boldness made a grand entrance, the unfamiliar kind that I once thought was uncomfortable.

Another defiant act involved the guitar, the instrument of the '60s and '70s. Everyone in school was learning to play it. Guitars were everywhere; even our music teacher sang with a guitar. However, I was forbidden to play the instrument because it was believed that playing the guitar would destroy my piano technique. Calluses would form on my fingertips and the abnormal strain from shaping my hand would be detrimental to my pianistic ways. I just wanted to try the easy-to-figure-out folk music of the day. So I found a way to play the guitar, again, at my friends' homes and in school. I learned to be resourceful.

My developing aural skills enabled me to learn the songs easily. The chords were simple, the tunes catchy, and the beat fairly regular. One particular song caught my attention in 1969. It was Richard Harris's version of "MacArthur Park." There was something about the orchestration and song structure that intrigued me; a bit more complex than the usual pop fare. By listening to the seven-to-eight-minute song each time it was played over the radio, I was able to figure out the entire song's chord progression and orchestration to play it on the piano, almost like a Romantic piece. I especially love the instrumental interlude. The cool song felt like a three-movement vocal symphony. Daddy, without a discriminating ear, wouldn't be able to tell if I was playing Pyotr Ilyich Tchaikovsky or Jimmy Webb, so I got away with practicing pop songs during practice time.

> I would gladly step back into the race of life because God reigns, no matter what!

During one of my piano lessons, Mrs. Brimo had to pause to take an important phone call. She asked me to continue playing and left the room. Five minutes became ten minutes. I was getting antsy. Mama was quietly reading in a corner of the room. I didn't want to play Liszt anymore, so I switched up to playing "MacArthur Park" with gusto. It was so much fun pounding the song on Brimo's grand piano like I was a rock star. I was about to get into the instrumental interlude section when Mr. Oscar Yatco, the Filipino Juilliard-bred violinist and orchestra conductor, walked into the room. I was flabbergasted, more like terrified, because I thought I was caught doing something wrong or outright forbidden in the classical world; worse, that I was stooping down to playing low-cultured music. The "MacArthur Park" indulgence came to a screeching halt like I'd seen a ghost. Well, I also had a crush on the handsome then 40-year-old Yatco so like a deer in the headlights, with my open mouth, I sat motionless. He approached the piano with a slight grin. He asked, "You figured all that out by yourself?" He had listened to a good portion of the song. "Yes, sir," I apologetically answered, complete with a raised pitch on "sir" as if I had been caught with my hand in the cookie jar. Where was my teacher anyway? She's been gone a long time. Mr. Yatco moved towards the piano bench. His grin now showed some teeth. In a mischievous tone, he quipped, "You're about to get to my favorite part; go on, keep playing."

I suddenly lost all sense of decorum at the piano. I launched into our shared favorite interlude section with its rhythmic, syncopated drive, cool circle progressions, and dynamic motivic phrasing. I pounced on the keys while my left foot tapped. I was so inappropriate for a classical musician. I sounded more like a piano player, not a pianist. But it was exhilarating. It was as though I had been granted permission to let go of all my inhibitions to play something totally outside my prim and proper persona. Before I arrived at the cadence, Mrs. Brimo walked in, wondering what the ruckus was all about.

Mr. Yatco beckoned her to come to the piano, "Stella, you didn't tell me Ruth could also play like this!" Like this. Like what? I never did ask him what he meant by "this." I was sure Mrs. Brimo did not have a clue I could play like that, whatever "that" meant. Anyway, I just wanted to have some fun. And I did. And I was thrilled my crush also joined in the fun! Mama? She just rolled her eyes.

I was also drawn to the music of the group Chicago and the dynamic horn arrangements of the rock/jazz fusion band. Their shared vocal leads were innovative and featured the different vocal timbre strengths of the group. The 1971 hit "Colour My World" naturally became a favorite with its piano accompaniment. Again, I figured out the chord progression by ear. More importantly, I also found a way to break up the monotony of my practice routine. I was not a young girl anymore. My teenage defiant side was emerging. It was probably more directed towards Daddy than anybody else, because of his controlling nature. He had been monitoring my practice from the same chair, the same desk, with the same fixed stance reading the *Manila Times* for more than six years. Nothing had changed. If I didn't get a break from him, then it would be all up to me to give myself a break.

I was studying the first movement of the Rachmaninoff *Third Concerto in D Minor,* a monster piece. I was becoming tired, so I shifted gear to something contrasting, a slower piece. I opened the pages of the Beethoven *Moonlight Sonata*. I was reviewing the first movement noted for its introductory broken chords, the right hand in ostinato triplets, and followed by the insertion of a drawn-out haunting melody slightly ringing above the triplet rhythm. The serenity of the movement, though steadily rhythmic from beginning to end, was the perfect respite from the power and bravura of the Rachmaninoff.

I was halfway through *Moonlight* when I decided to change up the routine. Either I was getting bored or maybe again I just wanted to have some fun. The first movement's triplet feel and tempo were identical to a pop song. You can probably guess where I am going with this. I took the bait. With a stroke of an improvised common chord modulation through a series of chord progressions, including secondary dominants (thank goodness for Saturday theory classes), I seamlessly arrived at "Colour My World," the latest pop song that fancied me. Daddy couldn't tell anyway if I was playing Ludwig van Beethoven or James Pankow. The triplet rhythm of both songs made it easy to fool Daddy. How did I know that he couldn't tell? He just kept on reading his newspaper. By then, it became more like a game. The challenge of each practice would be to figure out which classical piece best modulated to which pop song. Would I be able to trick Daddy, again? Where was Mama? She came down the stairs, tiptoed to the piano, gave me a look, waited till I got to the end of the song, and then motioned for me to stop the nonsense and move along. No words, just one look. It's time to leave Chicago. Fun interrupted. I proceeded with

Beethoven's second movement. Mama quickly disappeared as if she had never been there.

I not only loved to watch sports on TV, but I also loved to play sports. However, I was not allowed to play intramural sports in school. It's all about my precious fingers and risking a hand injury. However, I signed up for ICAM's intramural volleyball team in my freshmen year. I loved my teammates: Nits, our captain, Luisa, Lou, Beth P, Mardy, Lise, Tin, Celia, and Lynn. I just wanted to have some fun, something new to achieve. All the volleyball practice was during P.E. days. We wore our second set of uniforms. I did not tell the family I was playing volleyball. I took a gamble with my hands and fingers with every serve, block, overpass, freeball, you name it. A girl just wanted to have some fun.

While the family thought I was probably engaged in jump rope or basic calisthenics, I was playing volleyball. Our team won the majority of the games but lost the finals to the upper-classmen. However, we won the championship our sophomore year. Not one family member came to watch a game because I kept them in the dark. Fortunately, I only incurred a few minor injuries, which were not enough to sideline me from the game or from playing the piano. Occasionally, the ball would make contact with my face or nose, but I got away with a lot. I stopped rationalizing the decision to play. Yes, I lied. I was selfish and foolish, but I had lots of fun. That was the only time I ever played sports, so to this day, I'm still glad I got that one chance. The only regret I had was that no one came to see me play. Perhaps, if I had just been honest, the family would have come anyway, cheered, and applauded all the wins. But I seriously doubted it. My already short-lived sports career would have been snuffed out in a day. Too bad the basketball program started after I had already joined the volleyball team. The basketball team, with Belle, the captain, and Jopay, Edith, Flo, Lot, Maripaz, Menchie, Nini, Tes, and Annie, far outshined the volleyball players. They were the hot shots on campus since our freshmen year. Sadly, I left team sports altogether after ICAM. I was relegated to dance and fitness exercises in the gym during my last two years of high school at Newtown High in Queens, New York.

What About Boys?

I gained a reputation in the neighborhood as an overprotected piano princess that no one, especially a male human being under any circumstances, should dare approach. Good neighborhood teenage boys, not the *kanto* (street corner) boys, appeared to live by an unspoken rule fostered by the elders in the community—when young men and young ladies met in the streets and eye contact could not be avoided, a quick small nod of acknowledgment would suffice to show respect towards the young ladies. I did not experience the usual "boys will be boys" teasing or bullying, although secretly, I wished there was more of the teasing part around when I was growing up. It's as though boys were strictly forbidden to pester me or even look at me, out of respect to my parents and grandparents.

I, on the other hand, noticed them. Who wouldn't? Our neighborhood was teeming with tanned, good-looking

Filipino boys. A few of these handsome guys played basketball almost every day in our next-door neighbor's backyard. I had a perfect view just outside my second-floor bedroom window of the human menagerie. I peered out the window many times, more times than Mama would have liked to believe happened. I had a crush on a few of them, usually the tall, more athletic types. Didn't I say I loved basketball? I wanted to have fun, but I didn't know how to go about it. Too many watchful eyes. I regretted not having had a chance to mildly flirt with any of them. I maintained my annoyingly clean image. The guys probably thought that all I cared about anyway was the music career I was being groomed for. Little did they know, I liked them.

I think my first teen crush was Rey, Efren's older brother. Efren and I grew up together. I saw old photos of us dancing together and serving as flower girl and ring bearer at a family wedding. But Efren did not play basketball. Rey did. However, my parents thought that there might be a particular young man who would be the perfect fit for their princess. It was a boy who attended another church and was emerging to be a young leader in his youth group. I saw him every fifth Sunday of the month when youth groups from four city churches gathered for a joint worship service. He asked my parents' permission to begin calling me on the phone. I was around fourteen. He and one of his parents also paid for the expensive concert tickets to join Mama and me a few times at the symphony. Remember that we got in for free? The poor kid even took violin lessons. What was he thinking? That I would be his accompanist, a teenage musical duo in the making? No way. He's no match to the Mendelssohn whiz boy of the concert stage, my supposedly Mendelssohn stage sweetheart. Imagine, I could have been in an arranged marriage! That would not have been totally out of the realm of possibility, considering we're Filipinos. It was then that I realized that I was glad I might be going to America sooner, if possible.

6 | THE JUILLIARD YEARS

Entering the Pre-College Division of the Juilliard School constituted a two-part process. Mr. Mieczyslaw Munz, a beloved piano teacher at the Juilliard School and himself a well-known concert pianist and contemporary of Arthur Rubenstein, traveled to Southeast Asian countries scouting for young talents on behalf of Juilliard. He was an impresario who promoted Juilliard's academic programs. In the summer of 1972, Mrs. Brimo arranged for me to play in Mr. Munz's master class. I played the first movement of the Rachmaninoff *Piano Concerto #3 in D Minor*, quite an ambitious feat for a young pianist. More popularly known as the *Rach Third*, I had not yet performed any part of the concerto in public. One of Mrs. Brimo's college students accompanied me. This amounted to the first informal audition for the fabled music school. Before I even realized what was happening, I found myself preparing for my farewell recital at the University of Santo Tomas after receiving the invitation from Mr. Munz to attend Juilliard. I had just turned sixteen.

I left Manila in September, just in time for fall classes in the Big Apple. Upon arriving in New York, the second audition immediately transpired within two days. That round determined my scholarship award. Every bit of money helped. Uncle Mel and Auntie Gladys, who were already living in New York, also enrolled me at a local public high school in Queens where I would begin my junior year of high school. They took me on a shopping spree that same day to the closest department store, Alexander's, for some necessary school clothes: sweater tops, knit mini-skirts, knee-high socks, low-heeled pumps, and a comfortable, light coat. Judging from my clothing, you would think I was attending parochial school again instead of a New York City public high school. Alas, I discovered right away on my first day of public school, from the steps leading to the main entrance door of the building, that perhaps I was overdressed. The public high school dress code appeared to be blue jeans, a white T-shirt with a hoodie sweater, preferably navy blue, and sneakers. It was a big culture shock! I felt the cool autumn air settling in, much cooler than what I was accustomed to, even cooler than December and January in the Philippines. Every wind gust ran chills through my bones. Knee-high socks brought a new sensation. I grew up in 88-degree weather all year round! A jacket, light as it was, was cumbersome but a welcomed accessory to my spiffy attire. I was a few days late in high school but right on time at Juilliard.

The Juilliard School began as the Institute of Musical Art in 1905, with the purpose of providing European-style conservatory training to Americans. The school was first housed at Fifth Avenue and 12th Street. In 1969, the school moved to Lincoln Center, a multi-building complex built on 16.3 acres of land west of Central Park. The Pre-College Division was also established the same year to provide intensive musical training to talented 8- to 18-year-old students. The first building of the complex, the present Avery Fisher Hall, was completed in 1962. Other buildings subsequently followed.[1]

First Solo Trip to Juilliard

The first item on the agenda during my first morning in NYC was to practice commuting to Midtown Manhattan from Queens via the subway. Uncle and Auntie insisted I quickly learn the ins and outs of the underground and adapt to the fast-paced routine of riding the trains and catching the bus connection. This was repeated the day I auditioned for the scholarship, but that was it. I was entirely on my own the following day.

I thought I could handle it—my first subway ride to Juilliard, alone! After successfully maneuvering the four-train changes, I missed my stop. First-time jitters, I guess. I failed to get off the train on 66th Street. After the last passenger on the train car stepped out, the doors began to close, and that's when it hit me—that was my stop! What was I thinking? Panic set in as the train slowly accelerated to head for the next stop, 72nd Street. Baffled by my lapse in concentration, which was not like me, and even more anxious that I was going to be late for my first piano lesson in America, the sudden realization that I was 180 feet underground compounded the unsettling claustrophobic feeling. I got off at 72nd Street station, now in panic mode. Where's the sky? I needed some air! How about street names? Intersections were nowhere to be found! I could have had at least some bearing if I were standing on the more familiar above-ground pavement. But instead, the decision to go uptown or downtown in the belly of New York City tested my sense of direction.

Standing frozen on the platform, I was in a quandary about which stairs to take to transfer to the correct train that would drop me back off at 66th Street. I did not want to be late. I did not want to end up in Harlem one way or Chinatown the other way. To play it safe, I decided to take my chances on the streets. I bolted to the first available staircase to take me to yet another platform to exit through the turnstile to run up another set of stairs to get out of the dungeon. Ah, what a relief it was! I did not care whether it was the polluted air that greeted me outside, the honking taxi cabs, the squealing sirens, the white clouds floating and peering through majestic skyscrapers, or just good plain sunlight. At least now I could see which way to go back downtown. I decided to walk my way back to 66th Street, well, I half ran and half walked the six long blocks. There was no way I was going to be late for my lesson!

Filipinos are notorious for being late. Ten o'clock, in Filipino time, means eleven. You can be late to a Filipino wedding or any event and still be on time. I used to wonder if my family was, indeed, Filipino. To not be punctual did not ring a bell among us. Being late was not part of my family's DNA. The importance of being punctual at all times was ingrained in our minds. Allow extra time in case you get lost, or miss your stop. If you are right on time, you are already late. Arriving at least 30 minutes ahead of schedule is better. I ended up making it to the door of the piano studio with 15 minutes to spare.

The Juilliard Aura

The Juilliard School appeared new and modern. Since its early days, Juilliard sought to set up security measures to guard and protect the institution's clientele. One had to show a valid student or faculty ID card to get through the front lobby. The lobby of the building was more indicative of a corporate building entrance, not a school or college lobby. Past the guards, elevators transported students and faculty to different floors where instruction in the performing arts of music, dance, opera, and drama was conducted. I got off the wrong floor one time, and I ran into aspiring, delicately lithe ballerinas on the floor, tying their ballet shoe ribbons in their pretty tutus and signature donut bun hairdos. I caught a glimpse down the hallway of the all-in-black, leotard-clad, modern dance students warming up before a class session. As an instrumentalist, I had a snooty attitude towards dance, drama, and opera. I referred to them as the more ostentatious performing arts, wherein the more prima donna artists resided. I always felt comfortable and safe in the purely instrumental classical environment I grew up in, an environment that promoted the illusion that we were the more "normal" variety. However, the truth was that one cannot fully escape the eccentricities that plague an artist, regardless of the type of artist or the medium of the arts. I know; I have my eccentricities. For the longest time, though, I refused to believe that I might be peculiar after all.

The facility was lavish. Thick carpets covered the floor along the hallways that went well into the privacy of each teaching studio and each practice room. Common areas on each floor doubled up as study halls or cool hangout places, a far cry from the typical college cafeteria or student union building lounges of the '70s. The gathering places resembled upscale hotel lobbies with multiple seating areas holding large-cushioned, comfortable sofas and coffee tables. An air of professionalism permeated the building. I don't ever remember any loud chattering. Instead, students discussed theory assignments or technique fingering in a hushed tone. On occasions, a teacher and student lingered in the hallway after the lesson to expand on what was covered in the class session. Colleagues cordially greeted one another. Despite the artists' competitive nature, people were civil towards each other, not overly friendly, but reserved and respectful.

The practice rooms, about 84 of them, all contained Steinway grand pianos. It is reported that to date the Juilliard Building houses between 250-270 Steinway grand pianos, the largest collection of Steinways in any one given place. I spent many hours in the practice rooms. As soon as the bell rang to signal the end of the school day at my regular high school, I quickly had lunch. Then, I hopped on a bus, took the subway, and after several transfers, I walked up the exit stairs on West 66th Street, heading straight to the practice rooms. I usually arrived at least an hour and a half before my Wednesday afternoon lesson.

The soundproof rooms made it easy to concentrate. A no-distraction zone was intentionally created for the serious music student. A kaleidoscopic motion of frenzied emotive playing or a flurry of technical brilliance in differing tempos or the cascading but recognizable Romantic or Impressionistic melodic lines paired with rich chromatic chord progressions emanated from every room. It's a myriad of sonorities, stunningly punctuated and coming together in a kind of harmonized resonance, a feast for the aural senses. It reminded me of the glorious sound in a concert; the quintessential orchestra tuning to Concert-A pitch, a seemingly noisy chaotic exercise but all coming to a symphonic unison. Every musician in the practice rooms would be focused and embrace a no-nonsense attitude. It was all business. I don't recollect anyone leisurely sight-reading a new piece. The fine-tuning, memorization, and perfecting of each running passage were the regular agenda of the long hours of practicing. Each practice was headed somewhere toward a run-through with the teacher, a jury examination, a class performance, or a recital.

Piano teaching studios held two Steinway grand pianos, one for the student and the other for the teacher. Going to my weekly piano lesson resembled a solemn ritual, one that rolled out in slow motion in my mind often to this day. From the practice room, I took what felt like a formal procession to my teacher's room. I was nervous each time, though thankful I did not have clammy hands. I entered the studio sanctuary in reverent silence, apprehensive, eager, and focused on the session. I walked towards the Steinway to the right, either a sympathetic friend or a hostile foe that day, depending on how well-practiced or ill-prepared I was for the lesson. I respectfully acknowledged my teacher, Mr. Munz. His words were few. But they would become increasingly accented as he ushered me into an hour-long lesson that was all at the same time intense, meticulous, demanding, reflective, stressful, nurturing, eye-opening, and extremely tiring. I learned early on that Juilliard was not for the faint of heart. The competition was fierce. There was always someone more talented than you, more prepared, more disciplined, and more wired for this lifestyle. You had to be a relentless warrior, fearless to face the battle and hopefully emerge victorious at the top of one lesson, one class performance, and one concert at a time. Then the cycle was repeated—again and again and again.

> Despite the artists' competitive nature, people were civil towards each other, not overly friendly, but reserved and respectful.

Saturday Classes

Saturday classes were between 9:00 am and 3:00 pm. Some of my unforgettable memories at Juilliard were of Ms. Frances Goldstein, my theory and keyboard studies teacher. My best estimate, as I remember it as a teenager, Ms. Goldstein appeared to be in her 60s. Anyway, she was, without a doubt, old-school. She stood and welcomed us to each class in the front of the classroom with a lit cigarette. If second-hand smoke was ever deemed dangerous to our health back then, no one dared utter it. I just adopted a grin-and-bear-it attitude, even though I was borderline asthmatic. The keyboard studies class consisted of six to eight students, each sitting at a piano, busily tackling clef and intervallic transpositions at the piano assigned on the spot or realizing the figured bass of Bach Chorales. Ms. Goldstein would write several chord progressions on the chalkboard. With each stroke of her trembling hand, she formed the note of each voice of the four-part harmony exercise. We eagerly anticipated the completed phrase, each chord progression shooting out of her brilliant mind with no notes in view anywhere. We shaped our fingers to play the exercise on the air piano before we executed the chord progression on the piano with the correct fingering. That was the easy part.

Following the initial reading of the exercises, we were then expected to transpose each of them to different keys with voice-leading sensibility and at a moderately fast speed. I have fairly good aural skills to be able to play pieces by ear and change the key of a song to suit the range of a vocal soloist at church. However, Ms. Goldstein's class confirmed that the honing of this one skill was necessary to take that which might have come to me naturally to the next level. I learned that later on it might be the difference between getting a job or not. This particular keyboard class was for pianists only. The competition was nerve-wracking. Cut-throat was

Each practice was headed somewhere toward a run-through with the teacher, a jury examination, a class performance, or a recital.

more accurate in describing the atmosphere on several levels; it was merciless and relentless, especially among instrumental peers. All of us expected to emerge on top alone, far ahead of the next person or the one behind us.

Group piano meant we played as a group and then, individually, when called. In the group performance exercise, any misstep, any out-of-sync execution or wrong note could prove humiliating. This seldom occurred, but it still did. I could only speculate that each pianist practiced the keyboard assignments at least 40, 50, or 60 times over to guarantee success at each attempt. But the solo check-up was a different story. A student's mental state may easily deteriorate from confidence to anxiety attacks within seconds. Though our exterior might not have indicated any hint of nerves, who knew what sort of mind-over-matter battle went on in our stomachs, hands, and shoulders? Ms. Goldstein was quick to call out a mistake. A swift terse ego-deflating correction was to be expected. An occasional sarcastic remark might be thrown in to cause the fear of God to descend upon each student, whether one believed in God or not. No one ever wanted to be in that position. Unfortunately, not one of us escaped embarrassment.

From the minute we entered the piano lab, we quickly turned into killer sight readers and theory gladiators. There was no way any of us would be foolish enough to come unprepared. I believe we practiced the most for this class because we either survived or died! We marked our territory —the piano console to which we were assigned. The students rarely looked at one another. There was no time to empathize with whoever was going to fall that day. We were mortified and compelled to concentrate on the task at hand. Trained to utilize our heightened sense of hearing, we glued our eyes to the chalkboard as we followed Ms. Goldstein's long stick through each chord progression. Our fingers navigated the piano keys, fully dependent on our developing tactile skills. No one was to look down at the keys. It was one of the most difficult classes I have ever tackled, but to this day, the highest return on investment. I can say that if anyone wonders why I am the kind of musician that I am today, it's because of Ms. Goldstein. Desired outcomes were deeply rooted in the foundational skills developed by her world-class teaching.

You had to be a relentless warrior, fearless to face the battle and hopefully emerge victorious at the top of one lesson, one class performance, and one concert at a time.

I also recall that Ms. Goldstein relished the preponderance of calling on me in class whether to answer a question or to demonstrate an exercise. That was the reason I diligently practiced for the class every day. I took on a "do-not-fail" attitude. Only a fool would risk coming to class believing one could extemporize. Her classroom setting was not the place for wishful ad libitum. Ms. Goldstein called us by our last name. She pronounced my surname *Toh-páh-chee-óh*, not *Toh-páh-see-óh*, as it should be. The thought occurred to correct her mispronunciation, but only for a fleeting moment. I imagined every Goldstein-response scenario on a continuum from mild audacity to complete disrespect. So I just let it be. I thought she transformed my name into something more artsy. It sounded like I had an Italian name, rhyming with Michelangelo and Caravaggio, and that was fine by me. I was secretly pleased.

I was not the nervous type when it came to performing, but Ms. Goldstein's class sessions tested my resolve. In my entire musical career, I was the most nervous when I sat in her class. However, I would like to humbly think that I performed well in Ms. Goldstein's class because I did not receive the brunt of her harsh criticism, unlike a few of my classmates. On the contrary, I noticed that she managed to send a slight grin or a nod of approval my way for every correct quick answer I called out or played. That was enough for me. I gleefully realized something—I might have been a teacher's pet!

Perfect Pitch

I did not know that I had absolute pitch, more commonly referred to as perfect pitch, until I came to Juilliard. My solfège and ear training teacher, Mr. James Wimer, could easily tell who possessed it or not. We not only sang as a group, but each student had to sing alone to be evaluated for matching pitch, interval identification, and solfège reading. Discovering that I had this weird ability was a pleasant surprise. It explained why and how I could easily identify not only single pitches as a child, but also chords and tonal clusters later in the ear-training classes at St. Paul's Conservatory. I also learned that I have relative pitch—the ability to compare notes to a reference note and recognize interval relationships. Although the advantages of having a perfect pitch or near-perfect pitch far outweigh the disadvantages, I often wondered what it would have been like to not have it at all, thereby having to rely on sharpening my relative pitch ability. At Juilliard, from what I remember, having a near-to-perfect pitch was more the norm. It was not such a big deal. However, to have perfect pitch was never enough.

If you want to check a pitch or tune a guitar these days, you turn on the electronic tuner. But back in the day, old-school teachers further honed our skills by requiring students to work with tuning forks. This was the case with Mr. Wimer. He required that we buy our own tuning fork, which was used as a standard of pitch to tune instruments. It was also going to be the reference point for our sense of pitch. It was not enough to work with a piano, for a piano could be out of tune. So, I worked with a tuning fork pitched on Concert-A every day, anywhere, and anyhow. I inserted the task into my daily schedule while doing homework, reading a book, or riding the subway. My commute to my lesson was about 45 minutes, so I made good use of that time. No big deal: hit the fork on your lap, listen to the pitch, hit it again, just keep listening to the pitch, hit the fork again, then match the pitch with your singing voice. I did this repeatedly. Such a strange ritual, but necessary if you want to be the best! Because I already had a near to absolute pitch, it was acceptable to just sharpen that one pitch, to make sure it was centered. I remember another student who bought seven tuning forks for each note of the solfège. Poor guy!

I do not remember the names of my fellow piano competitors. It was almost expected that one couldn't be on good terms or on a friendly basis with your classmates. The only pianist with whom I managed to have a semi-professional acquaintance was Pinky Amado. She's a Filipino pianist who was a child prodigy herself. She and I studied with Mr. Munz. She was in the College Division; I was in the Pre-College program. Occasionally, our lessons would be scheduled back to back. She was kind and friendly to the newbie. I searched for some semblance of friendships at Juilliard, but I discovered that such liaisons could be cultivated, yes, but only with non-piano students. I met David Bayard, a clarinetist, and Susan Rotholz, a flutist, both in Mr. Wimer's class. David and Susie were extremely talented but easygoing, kind-hearted, and friendly; quite a departure from what I was experiencing with my theory and keyboard classmates. The ear training class was another enclave of talented young musicians. It was a relief to finally have made friends in what otherwise would have been a rather lonely place for me. We were in the same class for two years. A few years later, we all found ourselves together again in the music department of Queens College. David and I were assigned to play a duo in a chamber music class. Susie and I, with a violinist, Claudia, performed as a group of soloists for the Bach *Brandenburg Concerto Grosso #5*.

I crossed paths with a former Filipino violin prodigy, Julian Quirit. I met Julian at ICAM when I was fourteen, where he performed one of several recitals in the community. He studied with the distinguished violinist, the late Ivan Galamian. I remember running into Julian almost every week on his way to his private lesson, and I from my own. He carved a successful performance and teaching career in Australia. Who knew I'd be hanging out with a future orchestra conductor? The Juilliard years proved to be the most compact years of my life. I learned so much in such a short time. The Juilliard experience was glorious beyond any imagination. I was able to call upon my established good habits of practice and discipline to help me face the challenging level of study with confidence to enjoy the experience. I am forever grateful for the blessing.

7 | WHY TEACHERS MATTER

It is common practice in music study to seek the tutelage of a particular teacher. Depending on the stage of development, a student may benefit from the strength of one instructor at a particular age and that of another at a later time. Studying with the same teacher longer, especially with an expert in the field, is also more conventional to acquire as many advanced skills and techniques as possible. It is a kind of submission to a discipleship or mentorship relationship that is considered invaluable and intangible. Therefore, in most cases, the institution plays a lesser role in the student's greater aspiration to study under an esteemed noted instructor. But, certainly, when the teacher is associated with a prestigious institution, the privilege becomes exponentially magnified.

"To teach is to touch a life forever" is a favorite teacher-appreciation quote attributed to Jerry Whittle, author and well-loved English and Braille teacher. The following is an attempt to honor a few rock-star teachers who have imparted their expertise and wisdom. They were rock stars in the literal sense, perhaps unknown to the general public, but in the classical world, these teachers were performers, pedagogues, composers, and theorists who left their mark on the concert stage, music institutions, and music business. They were highly respected among their peers. My much younger self often took for granted the rare opportunity that I had been given.

Reflecting on the numerous opportunities I have received, I can say now that the once-prodigy in me and my current teaching aptitude and competencies are beautifully reconciled to bring honor to the folks who have formed me into who I am today. Dr. Daniel Overdorf, Johnson University's President, describes in a sermon titled "Finishing the Sojourn Well," "If you reflect back on the life that you've lived up to this point, my guess is that as you reflect, what comes to mind most are names, and the people and the faces whose identities hang on those names. On every name there hangs a story—there hangs an identity."[1] I felt compelled to list a few names. I am thankful for the opportunity to put into words what these names have meant to me. The following are the stories of my teachers in the United States. The names and stories of the gifted men and women who shaped me in more ways than one.

Mieczyslaw Munz

I studied with Mr. Mieczyslaw Munz (1900-1976) at the Juilliard School Pre-College Division in 1972-1974. Mr. Munz was a concert pianist and a contemporary of Arthur Rubenstein. He was originally from Poland, and by age twelve, he made his debut in his native Krakow performing the Tchaikovsky *Piano Concerto #1*. Shortly after he studied in Vienna and Berlin, according to Krzywicki, Mr. Munz made his "New York Debut in 1922 in Aeolian Hall."[2] Aeolian Hall was a 1,100-seat concert hall in Midtown Manhattan, built in 1912 and closed down in 1926. Formerly housed by the Graduate Center of the City University of New York between 1961-1999, it now houses the College of Optometry of the State University of New York. After 20 years of Munz's concertizing with all the major orchestras in the United States and European capitals, Krzywicki added, "a severe nervous disorder of his right hand cut his career short."[3] He spent his last 30 years teaching only. "Munz's longest tenure was at the Juilliard School of Music where Emanuel Ax was his most famous student. A Munz recital always contained Chopin. He was acclaimed by critics for performing the rarely performed complete Chopin 24 Preludes."[4] Munz was already living in the United States when World War II broke out, but his family suffered the horrors of Nazi rule in Europe. Mr. Munz passed two years after I left Juilliard.

I remember Mr. Munz as serious and businesslike. He was already in his 70s when I studied with him in New York. He was bigger than life. He traveled to the Philippines and other Asian countries as an impresario, looking for young talents. I met him in Manila. Mrs. Brimo had arranged for me to play in one of his master classes after I had just turned sixteen. I was to perform the first movement of the Rachmaninoff *3rd Concerto*. A master class is a lesson offered to students of a particular discipline, usually music, by an expert in that discipline. You play for a master musician, and then a critique follows the performance. Corrections and

My much younger self often took for granted the rare opportunity I had been given. suggestions are made, like in a piano lesson, except that the class is in front of fellow music students, teachers, graduate students, and the invited public. Participants are placed on the spot and are expected to apply the corrections immediately.

Mrs. Brimo had arranged several master classes over the years, conducted by other visiting artists, in which her students would perform. I knew what to expect. I had sat in the audience before. I had seen the gladiators take the bench. A master class was tougher than a jury examination or an audition. I was prepared to arm myself with a degree of resilience for the kind of brutal critique and, sometimes, the hard-to-take "you-suck" comments that may follow an already gut-wrenching experience. It's more like a glorified piano lesson. A master class is a showcase venue, whereas a piano lesson is an intimate experience—one-on-one with your teacher. You diligently practice for a piano lesson, perhaps five to six hours a day all week, with hopes to come to your lesson to please your teacher and demonstrate what you have worked on all week long. The meticulous practicing that develops your technique and musical interpretation daily prior to each lesson is what pays off in the long run. I've been learning that good practice bears good fruit, and it is this good fruit that a student ambivalently takes to a lesson to hear the words, "Well done today."

The intense public scrutiny of a master class is a different story. You have to possess nerves of steel and quick thinking to immediately, on the spot, apply the suggestions by the master musician after the initial performance. That was my introduction to Mr. Munz. The concerto, one of the most technically difficult pieces in the piano repertoire, was fairly new to me. I remember how I marveled at how he painstakingly coached me to bring out the inner voices of the melodious passages. I did not know about the chromatic contrapuntal texture of Rachmaninoff's compositions at the time. Mr. Munz showed me the piece's depth and beauty in minutes. After an arduous session, he told my teacher that he was willing to take me as his student. Within a few months, I enrolled at Juilliard in New York.

Mr. Munz taught me how to play fast and furious but with laser-like precision. He worked on my technique. He quickly identified my weaknesses. He had an exercise solution to every fingering problem. Mr. Munz believed that the foundation of the seemingly effortless sweeping and lightness of fingers across the keys was the mastery of technique, rooted in the correct fingering of each passage. He meticulously wrote the fingering himself, writing in bold blue pencil, for each difficult passage of every piece he taught me. One thing Mr. Munz was intentional about was insisting not to waste every opportunity to use the ring 4th finger of each hand in running 16th-note passages. There was no argument to his process because his fingering worked. Mr. Munz was a specialist in technique development.

Alan Walker noted in *Reflections on Liszt* that Franz Liszt, the flamboyant rock star-like 19th century pianist had been a pupil of Carl Czerny. Czerny stated, "Because the fingers possess different characteristics, so the theory goes, it must be a function of the teacher to equalize them."[5] Therefore, after Mr. Munz identified the passages I had to clean up, unmistakably noticeable, marked in bold red pencil, he walked me through an elaborate but repetitive set of exercises to solidify the equal treatment of fingers; something that Czerny would have probably done himself. It's a finger workout like no other. His procedure would include varying the emphasis of accented notes, focusing on grouping the notes in pairs, and repeatedly but slowly building strength of each pair of two fingers, much like the boring Hanon exercises. In addition, Pischna and Moscheles technical studies dominated my practicing hours. There was no escaping the prescriptive pathway to mastery of technique.

I am amazed today at the arsenal of exercises I have been able to pull out and impart to my students to tackle technical difficulties. My students are equally awestruck as I was when I was a student, when the exercises worked almost instantaneously within minutes during the lesson if executed correctly and at a slow tempo. My former piano students can attest to the fact that it works like magic. I love the I-can't-believe-it-worked grin or the wide-eyed, toothy smile when the student has a light-bulb moment. I am satisfied to know they indirectly benefited from Mr. Munz's technical expertise. Paterson explains that after a season "the soil of your life is prepared to receive information and acquire skills," and our parents give us a foundation of esteem and worthiness, the next phase is "the school and college or vocational training years in which . . . valuable seeds are planted in you."[6] I'd like to think that I have made a difference in a student's musical development in this way. Forming the good habits to cultivate these seeds is key to materializing the talent one receives. It is not easy. It takes dedication. It is, indeed, inevitable that "Mastery is not a matter of wishful thinking. Mastery is rooted in practice and more practice and still more practice."[7]

Mr. Munz was sensitive to the fact that during the time I was attending Juilliard, I was living with my uncle and aunt and her mother in a two-bedroom apartment on the fifth floor of a six-floor building in Queens. There were neighbors above us, below us, and around us. Mr. Munz realized that practicing would be a problem in that environment. Apartment living is a way of life in New York City. My best friend, Beth Cruz, lived in a housing unit of a high-rise building. Imagine residing on the 21st floor like her family did! Beth and her sister, Louella, were taking piano lessons, as well. They faced the same predicament I did about practicing. But there was always a solution to address the unique challenges of city life. To solve the noise problem, Mr. Munz, early on in the first semester, handed me a folded burgundy-colored cloth. It was the size of a large blanket made of felt, not too thick, not too thin. He instructed me to lift the lid of my Baldwin Acrosonic spinet and lay the cloth across between the strings and hammers to muffle the sound. It was a seemingly archaic approach, but worked effectively so I could put in the hours without aggravating the neighbors. Mr. Munz looked out for me so I could succeed in my circumstances.

On a few occasions, I commuted to his Manhattan home for my piano lesson. Even as an adult, I seldom sauntered into the more affluent part of the city. I was intimidated because it took me out of my routine. Mr. Munz's apartment felt like a hallowed space for a ceremonial rite, much like his Juilliard studio. Piano teachers are simply larger than life. Students worship the ground they walk on. So when I stepped off the elevator and walked in the hallway leading to his door, just like the school hallway, I would be in the zone—focused and reverent. The lessons at his home seemed surreal. I remember shelves upon shelves of music books and other reading material, a great number of them open, music sheets scattered all over his teaching studio. The space intriguingly resembled an artist's domain. My obsessive-compulsive tendencies kicked in. I couldn't escape my first thought, "He needs a housekeeper." He probably had one.

I remember a story Mrs. Brimo related about Mr. Munz before I left for New York. Mr. Munz's divorce from his wife, Aniela Mlynarski, after a short marriage, made the news back in the day. She was the "daughter of Emil Mlynarski, founding conductor of the Warsaw Philharmonic and director of the Warsaw Opera. Her father introduced her to [Arthur] Rubenstein backstage after a concert."[8] She eventually married Rubenstein. I wouldn't presume that I had any idea how this might have impacted Mr. Munz. But the intuitive teenager that I was, I couldn't push aside my perception of him that what I first thought of as a serious business-like demeanor was, perhaps, a hint of sadness about a deep loss in his life. Mr. Munz never remarried. A hand injury ended his concert career. He dedicated his life to teaching thereafter. I treasure the memory of having been taught at his home. He was completely in his element, giving this student every ounce of his energy and focus, demanding and unrelenting.

Beyond my submitting to his authority in technique, Mr. Munz also guided me through a wide range of musical emotions, from the reserved yet delicately playful passages of a Mozart sonata to the frenzied symphonic-like sections of Beethoven's *32 Variations in C Minor*. He afforded me a front-row seat to delve into the melancholy side of Chopin as I studied the *Ballade #1 in G Minor*. The piece happened to be Mama's favorite. She asked me to sight read the piece when I was eleven. I indulged her. All she wanted was to hear the opening melody. I only played until page two each time she asked, as though I was waiting all along for the right time to study it. The right time was five years later with Mr. Munz.

Mr. Munz ushered me into the sophisticated balance of technical brilliance and subtle nuances in interpreting the sweeping melodic, harmonic, and chromatic structure of the Chopin *Etudes*. Mr. Munz treated the study of etudes like how you would study the *Czerny School of Velocity* and *The Art of Finger Dexterity*. Munz systematically assigned them, as a daily diet for finger exercises but with the intent of acquiring the technical ability to perform them with the same Chopinesque lyricism, subtlety, and brilliance as that of an *Impromptu* or *Ballade*. I must have studied half of the etudes volume. I probably would have finished all of them if I had stayed longer than the two years I studied under him.

Mr. Munz introduced me to a pedaling technique to enhance the color variances of the Ravel *Jeau d'eux* and *Sonatine*. He selected dynamic and showy pieces for study, which, on occasion, was a higher level of difficulty than I believed I could tackle at the time. He was a virtuoso. Listening to his recordings causes me to pause and wonder at the speed he performed the Mozart *Piano Concerto in D Minor, K. 466,* or the Rachmaninoff *Rhapsody on a Theme of Paganini.* He was a meteoric star in his prime. The fact that he dedicated most of his life to teaching turned out to be the highest privilege for those of us who had received the favor of a great maestro's tutelage.

While writing this chapter, I entertained a fleeting thought of contacting Munz's most famous student. Emanuel Ax, a multi-Grammy Award winner and Sony Classical exclusive recording artist since 1987, is the duo partner of world-famous cellist Yo-Yo Ma. I had no idea how to go about setting up an interview. It was a fortuitous possibility, the farthest chance of a long shot. I wrote down a few questions I had hoped to be able to, at the very least, send in an email. I debated if Mr. Ax would even entertain such a suggestion. Doing some research, I was able to successfully connect with Mr. Ax's manager. After a whole summer of my persistence and patience, his manager and her assistant graciously arranged a phone interview with Mr. Ax. It turned out to be so much better than an email interview.

Mr. Ax took a few minutes to answer my questions in the middle of his Midwest concert tour. We chatted about our dear teacher. When asked which two words best describe the strength and foundation of Munz's teaching, Ax said, "Practice habits. Mr. Munz believed in practicing slowly, in rhythm. Don't play fast. Good practice habits that would stay with you."[9] Mr. Ax's words confirm what Sterner wrote, "The paradox of slowness is that you will find you accomplish the task more quickly and with less effort because you are not wasting energy."[10] Every serious music student understands the simple advice.

After a brief mention of my rebellious years and how Mr. Munz advised me to continue my piano study with one of his Polish friends, Ax quickly countered, "I was not the rebellious type. I attended a lot of concerts. I heard the great pianists. I grew up in the tradition of imitation. Mr. Munz was the perfect teacher for me."[11] Mr. Ax confirmed, yet again, the importance of observing, listening, and even copying what established artists do. Whipple and Eckhart put it this way: "The single most important requirement for improving technique is to identify a standard or benchmark from which technical errors can be identified. Consider the difficulty a music student would have in learning a classic piece if he or she never were able to hear it performed at the highest level—a sound advice to students to consider improving technique simply by emulating the elites."[12]

Ax also noted, "Mr. Munz lived during the time of Rachmaninoff, Josef Hofmann, and Arthur Rubenstein."[13] At this point in the interview, I felt a lump in my throat. It caught me off guard. The implication of what he had just said suddenly hit me in a most profoundly solemn manner. I had pored over articles about Emanuel Ax and watched his video performances and interviews online. But the words of tribute, pouring out of a great concert pianist's mouth one afternoon, about a teacher whom we both deeply admired and respected, were words of affirmation of my musical journey. I wept silently, listening intently to his deliberately punctuated reflection.

Before Ax had to end our conversation to get ready for a Q&A session at a university concert hall scheduled that early evening, Mr. Ax concluded his homage to our beloved pedagogue. "Mr. Munz was a very great pianist who sadly had to stop playing because of his hand issue, but judging from a few recordings and the way he taught, he was very much in the grand tradition of Rachmaninoff, Hofmann, and Busoni. It was an incredible lineage—so lucky to have studied with someone like him."[14] The next evening, he performed a piano solo concert of Brahms, Chopin, Schumann, and Ravel, a repertoire set that I imagine our beloved teacher could have put together. I hope that in these few pages, I would have paid tribute, if only but a little, to Mr. Munz's legacy.

Rebellion, My Own Way

After Pre-College, I was set to continue into the college program. I did not have to audition again. I would just matriculate accordingly and continue studying with Mr. Munz. However, I decided to leave Juilliard to pursue a non-music degree. Mr. Munz was disappointed, to say the least, but quickly had a plan in mind. He strongly suggested that I contact Leon Pommers should I decide to return to music. Mr. Pommers was already teaching at Queens College where I planned to enroll. I abandoned my piano studies for two years after having been immersed in it for 13 straight years.

Rebellion did not manifest in experimenting with mind-altering marijuana or popping a hallucinogenic drug, which, around that time, was readily available in many parts of the Big Apple, probably even on the college campus. Rebellion did not lead me to hang out with what my elders would have called "no-good friends." I did not smoke or drink alcohol. I was a compliant teenager. My heart's uprising took on a form of stepping up and mustering the courage to defy my family's wishes of a concert career. I felt I carried the burden of the expectations of an entire village, my extended family, friends, and the influential Filipino music community who invested in me. However, coming to America meant I could be who I wanted to be, not who others shaped me to become. There was a serious inner battle for my talent and will. I realized I had to turn my back on the saturated musical life I've had. I was dripping wet and exhausted. I wanted some dry land to catch my breath. I wanted to be left alone to make one decision for myself.

Attending a liberal arts college made sense. I could take the required courses in my first two years. I was excited about the fresh start and some independence. Best of all, I did not have to practice for the first time since I was five years old. But though I deliberately tried to take out the music in me, I was drawn to the Queens College music department to take music electives. While I was taking required core freshmen courses, I told myself that for fun,

I could take music theory, sight singing, and ear training. For fun, I could sing in the college choir. For fun, I could play piano again. After I passed the vocal audition to join the ensemble and the music placement exam to take music theory and theory lab, for fun, I found myself hanging out with music majors and singing in the elite college choir to fulfill my electives. Students, music majors or not, who were taking the music theory sequence were also required to demonstrate proficiency on piano. So, guess what? I had to play in the required jury examinations. The music department became my haven and playground in the middle of the large city college campus I now had to navigate.

Several noted pianists were on the Queens College faculty roster. I remembered Mr. Munz's advice to contact Mr. Pommers, his friend and compatriot, a quiet man I'd only observed from a distance and whose students I'd heard perform. After I felt that I had rebelled enough, I naturally returned to music. I declared piano performance as my major at the end of my sophomore year. I requested to study with Leon Pommers. I did not know much about him. I just took Mr. Munz at his word.

Leon Pommers

"Sometimes a great pianist devotes the better part of an entire career to accompanying other great musicians, the soloists. That featured artist with whom the accompanist collaborates typically receives all the accolades, and the accompanist must be at ease with the fact that the public usually comes away from a concert remembering only the soloist. The 'billed' performer, however, could not have communicated an exceptional musical experience to the audience without a collaborator who complemented his or her abilities, musicality, and sensitivity. The accompanist may even bring his or her own ideas forward into the performance, leading the soloist to yet a higher level of musical interest. Such was the case with Leon Pomeraniec (Pommers), the leading collaborator of his generation."[15] Such was the description of my beloved teacher, Mr. Pommers (1914-2001), by Paul Kryzywicki from his 2016 book, a tribute to the hall of fame musicians who hailed from Poland.

Like Mr. Munz, Mr. Pommers was Polish. Kryzywicki recorded that Pommers was born in 1914 to "a well-to-do Jewish family in Pruzana—eastern Polish border with Russia" and that Pommers was "a boyhood friend of Menachem Begin, the future 6th Prime Minister of Israel."[16] Mr. Pommers was studying piano at the Warsaw Conservatory when World War II erupted in Europe. Germany invaded Poland. He lost his mother and a sister to the brutality of the Nazis, but Mr. Pommers escaped through Siberia, Japan, China, Australia, and Canada, then finally arrived in New York City. Subsequently, he taught and played at the Aspen Music Festival. "In 1962, at the Jazz Festival at Lincoln Center, he shared the stage with Eddie Burke, Lionel Hampton, Bobby Hacker, and Benny Goodman, not to play Goodman's jazz, but to showcase Goodman's affinity for the classics. Pommers accompanied him in Beethoven's Clarinet Trio. At the same time, they recorded the Beethoven and Brahms trios for a CD that also featured the Weber Quintet by the Berkshire String Quintet. When the recording was finally released in 1987, it was nominated for a Grammy Award."[17] Pommers was also the longtime accompanist of Nathan Milstein, Erica Morini, and Yehudi Menuhin.

At our first meeting, Mr. Pommers and I mostly talked about his friend, Mr. Munz. I told him my musical journey from Manila to New York City. My first impression of Mr. Pommers was that he was a man of calm demeanor with a mix of joyful disposition, charm, and wit. I immediately liked him. I found him to be nurturing but with high expectations for what I was to bring to the lesson each week. I was confident that he would take me to the next level of piano knowledge and skills. One thing was for certain, more serious practicing was hovering on the horizon. Mr. Pommers became my piano teacher when I became a Bachelor of Music major, a four-and-a-half-year program. I declared my major at the end of my sophomore year. I knew I had a lot of catching up to do. Good thing I took those music electives since freshman year.

Although my first assignment was to tackle a Mozart *Sonata*, unbeknownst to me, Mr. Pommers was already planning a series of performances for me, including an all-Chopin solo recital within a year. Mozart and Chopin immediately became my daily practice fare: a Mozart *Sonata*, a Chopin *Sonata*, several *Mazurkas*, an *Impromptu*, and a *Scherzo*. The contrast in performance practices between the two composers ignited my analytical side, this time to carefully observe and apply the proper technique to the stylistic nuances of each composer. Bellman and Goldberg articulate, "Chopin's idea of finger independence also differed from that of his contemporaries, who, he wrote, mistakenly trained all fingers to be equally powerful. He relied on the shape of the hand to develop the strength of each finger for its best use: a supple hand, the wrist, the forearm, the arm, everything will follow the hand in the right order."[18] Mr. Pommers taught me how to play Mozart and Chopin by using the shape of my hand. Whereas I used to play instinctively, studying with Pommers opened up a much-welcomed next level of musicianship.

I now entered my young adult years. He invited me to paint on new canvases, exquisite sonorities, and stunning voice-leading coloring I did not realize I was capable of. He took me on a journey of executing delicate playing, as well as, delivering stirring impassioned performances and everything in between. I truly rediscovered the joy of playing piano because he set the example himself. He modeled how to embrace the process and the discipline, and then, just "go for it" at show time. Yes, he taught me Bach, Beethoven, Mozart, Schubert, Chopin, Schumann, Rachmaninoff, Bartok, and Ginastera, to name a few. But moreover, he pushed me to become more attached to the music, to find its substance, internalize it, and then connect it to who I am.

I was playing a Chopin *Mazurka* during one particular lesson. I quickly detected his frustration from his furrowed eyebrows that I was far from executing an acceptable interpretation. The lesson was all about the term *rubato*, specifically the Chopin *rubato.* Bellman and Goldberg explained it this way: "The rhythmic license Chopin used in playing the mazurkas was often termed a Polish or nationalist rubato, distinct from the contrametric and agogic rhythmic freedoms, though in all probability his playing was characterized by a free and shifting mix of all three."[19] This is at the very heart of playing Chopin. I completed two years of piano study with Mr. Munz and now Mr. Pommers, two Polish-born concert pianists. They both regarded Chopin with nationalistic pride. I was immersed in Chopinesque performance culture, to say the very least. If I were to play Chopin, I had better play it correctly and authentically. The regular understanding and common practice of playing *rubato* is to "rob" (from the Italian word *rubare*) the tempo of a phrase by slowing down the first few beats and then speeding up to catch up with the regular tempo. However, the Chopin *rubato* dictates that the left hand stays on a steady beat while the right hand plays the melody in a free, meandering pace, either early or behind, against the steady left hand. This usually occurs in the slower melodious Chopin passages.

Instead of having me merely mimic how he played a Chopin passage, Mr. Pommers taught me how to realize an interpretation that would honor the spirit of Chopin. And to play the piece from within the deep recesses of my maturing musical development. The Chopin *rubato* proved elusive. Mr. Pommers dished out his bag of tricks one by one. First, he articulated the kind of mood that he was after. I tried to grasp it but failed. He then sang the melody and even asked me to join him in unison to feel the ebb and flow of the tune, yet he was still dissatisfied with my musical response. Finally, he asked me to get up from the bench so he could demonstrate the phrasing. It was just one phrase. Unfortunately, I was too frustrated to try a third time. He stopped the lesson. I anxiously anticipated a gentle rebuke. After what could qualify as the longest 30 seconds of my life, he looked straight into my eyes. With his adorable Polish accent, he suggested, "Pretend in your mind that you are with your Filipino boyfriend."

He modeled how to embrace the process and the discipline, and then, just "go for it" at show time.

I didn't know whether to laugh or cry. My boyfriend was in college 400 miles away. All I cared about at that moment was to get through the lesson and be done with that Chopin *rubato* once and for all. Why would I want to think about my boyfriend at this time? I was not in the mood anyway. It also would only have been a distraction. Upon my teacher's surprising but calculated prodding, I refocused and resumed playing, held captive to pleasant thoughts of my boyfriend. Voila! It worked. I delivered a mixed Filipino-Polish rendition of a Chopin *Mazurka* which was what my teacher was looking for. I cannot say enough of the man. Mr. Pommers was brilliant in that kind of way.

Next to the concept of *rubato*, Mr. Pommers was passionate about the left hand. The melody of a piece, for the most part, is obvious. It is the main idea. It is usually played with the right hand. So, the tendency to accentuate the melody, to bring it out, is often stressed to developing musicians. The norm is to make the melody of the right hand prominent and play the left-hand accompaniment more softly. Leon Pommers altered my perspective of melody and accompaniment. His chamber music background brought a deliberate approach to push his students towards a heightened awareness and understanding that melody exists in relationship to each part of the composition, and perhaps the obvious is not the most important part of the whole. Having him coach two of my chamber music classes reinforced the concept. Whether it was tackling the Weber *Grand Duo Concertante* with a clarinetist or the Schubert *Military March* on four-hand piano, Pommers's ability to elevate each player's ensemble proficiency was flawless, clearly rooted in his vast experience as the partner of great musicians in chamber music repertoire.

"Pay attention to your left hand!" It was Mr. Pommers's mantra, day in and day out, during the first semester of lessons with him. Thus began my enculturation to a new world of treating a piano solo piece like an orchestral web of outer voice relationships and inner voice balances. Theory and analysis classes systematically highlight voice-leading relationships. I was learning all of that. But it's a different story when your piano teacher starts to shift your paradigm from the old practice that you have espoused all of your musical life to something more complex than just playing with your right hand and left hand. Pommers subscribed to the philosophy that the bass part is the foundation upon which music is built. Many bass players would be thrilled to hear this, something they have known all along.

When learning a new piece, contrary to the common approach to sight reading first with the right hand, Pommers insisted that I first play the left-hand part, the accompaniment. The next step was to isolate the bass notes. If there were multiple parts for the left hand, he suggested having the left hand play the single bass notes or octaves with more depth to let the bass notes ring. For the rest of the bass clef part, he would then have the right hand play those parts, left and right hand playing the accompaniment. I resisted it, insistent that it would be a waste of time to play left-hand parts with the right hand. But there was some method to the madness. After going through the exercise, I could then play the entire bass clef part as written for the left hand now with an acute awareness to play the accompaniment with the left hand as though two hands were playing the part. I asked, "What's the point of all the tedious process? When will the right hand be invited to the party?" I couldn't wait to get to the final results.

After the left hand fully dominated the first reading, the right hand finally got its chance. The melody's entrance almost became anticlimactic. The melody was the easier part of the left-hand and right-hand debate. Yet another step was added, which was to play the left hand alone and sing the melody. I wanted to skip this part because I did not consider myself a singer. So why should I bother singing the melody out loud? I could do that in my head. But again, I complied. So when I finally pieced together all the parts of the whole, something extraordinary happened. I started to hear much more in the music: the various layers of voice leading, the melody contrasting beautifully with the emphasized bass notes, and the balanced inner voices that flowed together like brushstrokes of light. It created a symphony of sonorous beauty, not played by an orchestra or chamber ensemble but by a pair of hands. So pay attention to your left hand! Mr. Pommers, you made me a believer.

The study of Bach's fugues presented yet another view of Pommers's teaching approach. I was fascinated by his insistence that beyond the reading of bass clef alone or treble clef alone and the meticulous fingering of the Bach fugues, one must play each voice in a deliberately slow tempo, each time gradually moving towards *a tempo*. Each voice, not each hand. Sometimes, the voice part switches from one hand to the other, and that could be tricky. What first appeared as a boring task of isolating the bass part, the tenor part, the alto, and the soprano while playing each part with the correct fingering and dynamics, in various tempi, from *slow* to *a tempo*, solidified the technique and assimilation of a difficult form of piano music. Pommers taught me to appreciate the Bach fugue for its polyphonic flow instead of the usual pedantic nature many misconstrue it to be.

Another concept strongly reinforced by Mr. Pommers was to develop restraint and self-control not to get stuck with mistakes along the way of any performance, even during a piano lesson. My early years of stage experience prepared me to internalize the philosophy. But it was Mr. Pommers's repeated reminder, "No matter what, don't stop. Take it to the end," that became so deeply ingrained in my psyche. He became the still, small voice that guided me through tricky live

"Pay attention to your left hand!"

performance situations and random loss of focus. Pommers regularly insisted on treating each run-through performance as *the* performance. Simultaneously, each performance allows practicing the reaction to any unexpected blunder or distraction during the performance.

In practicing for unforeseen mishaps, Gordon advises to "resist starting over or limit [the] indulgence . . . once such a habit gets entrenched, it is extremely difficult to break."[20] It is so true. It is necessary to have several run-throughs so that the "increased burst of energy will cause you to overreach yourself, and you will turn in a performance of such power and excellence that even you will be astonished. Gaining some experience in dealing with that adrenaline rush is of great value."[21] In retrospect, I understand now the value of Pommers's practice of inviting his colleagues to his students' private lessons. I had some sort of a regular test audience to observe the latest piece ready for performance. Occasionally, it would be impromptu; Mr. Pommers would grab someone in the hallway, any time during my lesson, the chairman of the music department or a composer colleague, a cello professor or a jazz trumpet professor, to come in and listen to my not-quite-ready-for-prime time viewing piece. Talk about being put on the spot time and time again. I was amazed at the intentionality of his teaching in this way.

One of the sweet things I recall him doing each year at

Christmas time was sending me a Christmas card in the mail with beautifully written sentiments. I wondered why he did so because he was Jewish, after all. Anyway, I remember him full of Christmas cheer each season. He was a family man. I got to know his wife quite well. About once every six weeks, Mr. Pommers arranged for a lesson at their home in Forest Hills, New York. Commuting to his house was not simple, but I looked forward to it every time. His wife would prepare hot tea and kolaczki cookies after the lesson. While nibbling on the goodies, I would solemnly look over the rows of family pictures meticulously positioned on the table, on the piano, and on the walls around the living room, mindful of the Pommers' heritage and his family's horrid experience during World War II. I became more intrigued about Mr. Pommers. Here's a man whose family suffered the worst kind of inhumanity against humanity. Here's a man who endured the hardship of escaping from his homeland to any country that would welcome him until he reached America. Here's a man who could have been embittered by his past. Instead, Mr. Pommers became an inspirational, caring teacher whose personal motto spurred his students to achieve their goals that no matter what, they should not stop; they should take it to the end.

I learned exemplary techniques from all my piano teachers, but Mr. Pommers taught me how to breathe in music and breathe out my soul. Ironically Krzywicki muses, "he never considered himself a pedagogue of the piano, but all who knew him valued him as a gifted teacher for his enthusiastic playing and coaching."[22] Pommers modeled balancing career and family. He taught me that I can have a music career, get married, and raise a family, too. He taught me how to rise above any circumstance. Mr. Pommers was the one who inspired me to become the teacher I have become, one who loves to teach and loves her students. To honor the passing of Mr. Pommers in 2001, Joel Lester, the then Dean of Mannes College of Music, expressed the following: "They don't

> **Mr. Pommers taught me how to breathe in music and breathe out my soul.**

make gentlemen like Leon Pommers anymore."[23] This I believe was Leon Pommers's secret weapon—that despite the hard challenges he faced in his lifetime, in all his collaborative endeavors with great artists, in his personal and professional relationships, and in his interaction with his students, he was first and foremost, the perfect gentleman.

Aaron Copland School of Music, Queens College

My education at Juilliard firmly anchored the strong foundational instruction I received at the St. Paul's College Music Conservatory in Manila. The no-nonsense, intentional, and intensive Juilliard approach to teaching technique and tone production, coupled with the rudiments of theory and musicianship, cradled my progress and, without a doubt, thoroughly prepared me for what was to come. On the other hand, Queens College (QC), where I received my bachelor's and master's degrees in piano performance, introduced me to an unfamiliar approach to music study. Up until I began studies at QC, much of what I learned about music centered on the performance. It was about the piano solo and orchestral performance, progressively moving from one piece to the next, one level to the next, and one concert to the next. The music degree program at QC was strongly complemented by a friendly, nurturing, high-quality academic environment of faculty, peers, and administration. It was a unique experience that baffled me for a long time because the college was in the borough of Queens. Everything top-notch had to come from Manhattan, so I thought. Here are the names and stories of the folks from QC.

Leo Kraft was an established American composer in the New York and international scene when I became an undergraduate student at QC. He hailed from Brooklyn, and studied at QC and Princeton University. His most noted composition teachers included Karol Rathaus, a German-Austrian Jewish composer who escaped Germany during World War II and eventually became a composition teacher at QC. Rathaus's works stemmed from the composition tradition of Gustav Mahler and Igor Stravinsky. Kraft also studied under Randall Thompson and Nadia Boulanger. Boulanger taught many noted composers and arrangers of the 20th century, like Aaron Copland, Elliott Carter, and Quincy Jones, to name a few. During my undergraduate degree, Professor Kraft gave me opportunities to play in chamber ensembles that featured new contemporary or modern music. He then formed a new venue in New York City for composers' work to be performed. His love for new music and his dedication to inviting young artists to perform was unparalleled.

When I returned to my alma mater to pursue the Master of Arts in Piano Performance, my first course was a *Baroque Performance Practice* seminar. It was taught by Raymond Erickson, an internationally recognized Bach scholar, harpsichordist, and pianist, who also taught at Juilliard. It was my first class in a while, so I was enthralled that I was studying under another master musician. Historical performance practice seminars quickly became my favorite graduate courses. I was thrilled that it was a performance class, something that was familiar. I was eager to get down to business and perform a few pieces in a master class-like setting. It was a breeze. Grad school was not bad at all, or so I thought.

Everything changed in the following seminar. Next in the sequence of courses was the *Pro-Seminar in Analysis and Style Criticism* taught by Professor Kraft. To say that he was a tough professor would be putting it mildly. Edward Smaldone described Kraft in this way: "His music had personality, like the man. It was spiky. It could be tart; it could be sweet. It could be fierce; it could be gentle. It was always intelligent; it always had a point of view. It didn't waffle or hedge. It was smart, confident, generous, and outgoing, and it always demanded careful attention. It wasn't easy."[24] Smaldone's words best described Leo Kraft.

For the *Pro-Seminar*, Professor Kraft required an analysis paper, five to six pages of text, each week. That was one of the most difficult course-related challenges I ever had.

His critique of my writing was harsh. Of course, this was graduate level, what was I thinking? I vividly remember his response to my first attempt. He entered his written corrections and suggestions on the typewritten pages and then tersely asked me to practically rewrite the entire paper. I was relieved more than anything for the reprieve—I got a chance to improve the paper another week before the next class. However, the ghostly form of the second research paper was looming over the following week. It suddenly dawned on my creative, non-analytical part of the brain that I would have to navigate through writing two seminar papers in fewer than six days. I was doomed to a never-ending sentence of writing critical analysis essays. Mind you, I had a ten-month-old baby and a toddler dominating my waking hours, plus a teaching studio to contend with. I seriously doubted my ability to get through the course. If hitting the wall was a legitimate description of what was happening in that class, clearly, I instantly hit the wall the second semester.

Somehow, logic prevailed. Again, I found enough prescriptive dosage from my cache of "no matter what" kind of tools. Deep down, I believed that I could get through the hump, finish well, and enjoy Kraft as a teacher who truly wanted me to succeed. He was that kind of a person. And so, slowly but surely, with progress each week in my writing, the confidence steadily emerged. I credit Leo Kraft with honing my writing skills. To the extent that I can say, because of his rather obstinate attitude in his teaching approach, Leo Kraft was the person who single-handedly prepared me for doctoral research and writing down the road.

I contacted Professor Kraft a few years before he passed away to thank him for his impact on my musicianship and capacity to pursue a doctorate, and that I feared him the most out of all my teachers. I reminded him how critical he was of my writing skills—how he unapologetically insisted each week to revise and elevate the essay to a more scholarly level. He graciously emailed me back. A small package later arrived with a signed CD of a collection of his compositions and a copy of *Partita No. 1* for piano solo. He wrote, "Of course, I was hard on you in the Pro-Seminar because I was hardest on the best students, and in spite of occasional complaints, I endeavored to maintain the highest standard possible." Additionally, Professor Kraft reminded me of why he became a teacher and why I became one, likewise. He continued, "The whole purpose of having a school is to benefit the students, and they are the ones who will gain the most from your efforts." Even towards the end, the ever-conscientious pedagogue did not fail to teach me that teaching is all about the students. What a stand-up guy! Edward Smaldone, in his tribute to Leo Kraft at Kraft's memorial service, said, "We have lost one of the longest-standing links to the origins of The Aaron Copland School of Music and one of the last living legacies of our tradition. We've lost a wonderful composer and a true champion of new music. But Leo was a staunch supporter of future generations of composers through the Leo Kraft Scholarship Endowment, which he established with a major gift just last year. His music and his generosity will continue."[25] Mr. Kraft, the pedagogue at heart, always had the student's best interest in mind.

Early in my college career, Professor Paul Maynard asked me to be one of his two choral accompanists. It was an unpaid assignment but more of a privilege. I accepted the invitation to gain more experience in choral accompaniment. Everyone said it would be an honor to work with Maynard. So, I did a double duty in Maynard's choir. To receive college credit, I auditioned and ended up in the alto section because I could sight read well despite possessing an untrained voice. Not only did I have to learn the vocal parts, but I also spent additional hours to learn how to play the isolated vocal parts and the piano accompaniment; anywhere from an orchestral reduction of the Mozart *Requiem* to the Brahms *Requiem*, Beethoven's *Ninth Symphony*, Stravinsky *Symphony of Psalms*, and George Perle *Songs of Praise and Lamentation: From the 18th Psalm*. I got to play some serious formidable music literature, but was quite oblivious to the significance of having these choral masterpieces under my belt. How I managed to practice difficult choral repertoire, in addition to my regular lesson and ensemble repertoire, boggles my mind to this day. I guess when you had to do what you had to do, a "no matter what" kind of situation—you just do it. After this kind of experience with Paul Maynard, I expected everything else to be easier, even *The Hallelujah Chorus*.

Dinu Ghezzo, a Romanian conductor and one of my theory professors, gave me a chance to perform the John Cage *Sonatina for Prepared Piano*. I had not heard of "prepared piano" before Ghezzo's assignment. I had read about prepared mustard in a recipe, so I was perplexed. The piano had to be prepared in some way. The whole experience started with the intriguing process of "preparing" the grand piano with erasers, bolts, metal nuts, etc., to alter the sound of the piano to sound like an Indonesian gamelan orchestra. The music score was quite specific: which foreign object to be inserted inside a piano, on which specific string, and from which distance. It was a tedious process. Ghezzo secured permission from the department to "prepare" one of two pianos in the recital hall. He and I worked on prepping the strings before each rehearsal, and then dutifully removing the hardware. Of course, the piano had to be tuned afterward. The live performance was a hit. It was recorded and played by DQXR in NYC. Ghezzo concluded his prolific career as Director of Composition Studies at New York University. Likewise, his wife, Marta Árkossy Ghezzo, rocked it as my ear training and solfège instructor for several semesters. She was meticulously precise. Her doctoral work resulted in a complete musicianship textbook. I subsequently adopted her book into the Music Theory Lab sequence at the university.

Professor Joseph Magnus Goodman, a pianist-composer and another theory professor, had a unique way of handing out keyboard assignments. In addition to playing the advanced chord progressions in different keys, Goodman required students to transpose two or three of the *Bach Two-Part Inventions* in at least three other keys on the piano. That was our keyboard requirement in the third semester of theory. He also taught students how to write two-part inventions. Somehow, I also managed to write a Bach-like fugue for a final project.

Morey Ritt, a venerable solo and chamber music artist, pedagogue, recording artist, and one of my chamber music coaches, assigned me to play the Primo part of the Rachmaninoff *Suite No. 2 for Two Pianos* with Elaine Chelton, also a student of Leon Pommers. Professor Ritt also invited me to be her graduate assistant. I taught a Group Piano Course of ten students, each on an upright piano (yes, ten uprights in a classroom). She came to observe and evaluate my teaching. I remember her encouraging comment at the end: "You will make a terrific teacher. You have an ease about you in the classroom." I did not consider college teaching when I was growing up. I knew I could handle teaching private lessons but not an entire music class. Morey Ritt planted that seed in my mind that bore fruit in subsequent years.

Carl Schachter, who also served in the faculty at Juilliard and the Mannes College of Music, gained international acclaim as the foremost expert in Schenkerian analysis, next to Schenker himself. He taught analysis and counterpoint courses at QC. I could not remember a day when I did not look forward to sitting in his classroom. I was mesmerized by his genius. His expressive piano playing to demonstrate each aspect of voice leading and melodic contour was beyond fascinating. Each class session was peppered with profound insights. Schachter's piano

Like scaffolding, teachers, during a specific period, temporarily support and guide students from one level to the next of learning.

demonstration evoked the essence of each period composer. But his interpretation of Beethoven sonatas, I loved the most. Sitting in his classroom one day, I made myself a promise that should I ever be blessed with an opportunity to teach music appreciation or music theory in the future, I would strive to be like Carl Schachter. That is, not to play a recording of an example, but instead, play the example on the piano with the same commitment I was to render at a stage performance.

In construction and renovation projects, scaffolding is the temporary structure that provides support for the materials and workers. Like scaffolding, teachers, during a specific period, temporarily support and guide students from one level to the next of learning. Students achieve competencies in their chosen field because of the help and mentoring they receive from their instructors. Teachers guide you for a season, then they get out of the way and charge you to succeed independently. Teachers matter. They educate, inspire, challenge, and motivate. They teach discipline and perseverance. They lead by example. Some of the names I listed above can be found in *Harvard's Dictionary of Music*. That's all I have to say about that.

> Teachers guide you for a season, then they get out of the way and charge you to succeed independently.

8 | MORE MUSINGS

Coming to the United States at age sixteen seemed like a slam dunk for glamorous and exotic living. It's what the citizens of numerous countries dream of. Leaving your parents and family behind in exchange for studying at the world's prestigious music school in New York City was both a dream come true and a daunting challenge for a foreigner. I was amazed at the diversity of the city. We did not call it diversity then. We'd say New York was a melting pot. Come to think of it, where else in the world could I, a Filipino, 1) live with a U.S. naturalized citizen/Filipino immigrant uncle who married a U.S naturalized citizen/Cuban immigrant woman; 2) become friends with Filipinos, Dominicans, Puerto Ricans, Cubans, African Americans, and Polish, Italian, and Irish Americans, Vietnamese, and many Jewish New Yorkers; 3) work with African Americans, Italian Americans, and Jewish ladies, 4) study with Polish-born piano teachers; 5) study under Jewish American professors and mentors; 6) attend a church that celebrated an International Day with an international luncheon each year; and 7) attend a church youth group led by a Midwest-bred youth minister amongst Chinese, Filipino, Ethiopian, Anglo-Saxon, and Afro-Trinidadian folks? I met my future husband, Elizur (Eli), at a musical production of *Godspell* at this particular youth group. He played John the Baptist. I was the piano accompanist. We met at the melting pot of the world. I couldn't have experienced anything like this in Manila. I say I love New York, but I'd say even more emphatically that I love the people of New York.

I thought Manila was busy, noisy, dusty, and overpopulated. New York City in the 1970s was even more frantic, absurdly bustling, and brash. Pollutants contaminated the air from the smog. Roads teemed with yellow cabs, buses, cars, scooters, bicycles, and pedestrians. Moreover, I haven't seen that many people congregate in the subway and pack shoulder to shoulder in the trains, an uncomfortable predicament for short people like me.

At street corners, a sea of humanity, dressed in business attire but in sneakers, mixed in with those clad in casual hobo style or chic glamor, waits for the traffic light to signal "walk" to synchronically cross the street. Everyone in the city appeared to be in a rush to get somewhere, except the occasional tourists in T-shirts and shorts, who interrupted the rhythmic flow of foot traffic. It was intimidating at first, but I quickly adjusted to the pace of life. One thing is for sure: I refused to stick out like a sore thumb. I learned to blend in and act like a native New Yorker. If dozing off in the subway and waking up in time to exit at your destination station counts, I've passed the test in becoming a New Yorker.

Fast Tempo Prodigy

Lang Lang is a former Chinese piano prodigy who achieved global success. Although he has been in the classical art music scene for a while, I really didn't care much for his playing because of his flamboyant hairstyle, wardrobe, and mannerisms. I watched a performance of Lang Lang with the New York Philharmonic Orchestra broadcasted live on TV on New Year's Eve in 2010. He played the Tchaikovsky *Piano Concerto in Bb Minor*, the same piece that trumpeted and solidified his place on the music concert stage when he performed it with the Chicago Symphony Orchestra in 1999 as a seventeen-year-old. Lang Lang was asked at the last minute to substitute for the artist, Andre Watts, who had to cancel. Lang Lang's fame shot through the roof since.

Lang Lang studied at the prestigious Curtis Institute of Music under Gary Graffman, yet another renowned concert pianist and teacher. Lang Lang dazzled the world with his dynamic performances. Still, he has his detractors and critics who blast his bravura style. The New Year's Eve performance caught my attention—such musicality, brilliance, virtuosity, lightning speed, sensitivity, and charisma. I finally paid attention to him. He demonstrated a mature playing and expressiveness that was of a master pianist. So I have been following his career: listening to his recordings, watching every Great Performance concert on public television, and watching his countless YouTube performances and master classes. He is a bona fide artist. Imagine the countless hours of practicing to perfect his craft. What we call discipline and dedication, Lang Lang takes to insanely off-the-charts proportions to be the best.

There is one trait that child music prodigies share. Lang Lang, now an adult, exhibits it, and so does Yuja Wang, an equally super-talented Chinese female contemporary of Lang Lang. I attended Yuja's formidable weekend marathon performance of all four Rachmaninoff piano concertos. What a grand experience for a fan! Both Lang Lang and Yuja are piano virtuosos who play pieces faster than usual. The ability to push the tempo that has already been marked *allegro* or *vivace* or *allegro vivace* is a trademark of a virtuoso. Play a piece as fast as you can take it. One can only imagine what *presto* means to a piano whiz. To taste a thrilling rush of adrenaline by bolting the stated tempo of a musical piece to a speed that oftentimes defies logic! Why not? Well-disciplined, youthful fingers can move more fluidly and rapidly across the keyboard. Couple that with the kind of juvenile vigorous energy that is innate in younger performers, clearly, no extra help from a booster energy drink is required. The quest to test your tempo limits is so seductive. Almost every young artist succumbs to the temptation and occasional detriment of performing with a less expressive interpretation of the music. Fast-tempo playing is a kind of restless, euphoric fix.

Teachers expect it. It all starts with how fast you can play your scales and arpeggios. How fast and how flawlessly clean, that is. Pushing the tempo limits is what makes a prodigy's performance more fantastical and sensational, with a kind of execution that fuels the wow factor. What a young talent lacks in interpretation and meaning, they make up with tempo bravura. On the other hand, it is safe to say that a restless young performer may not conquer the slower second movements easily. Second movements are more of the slow variety, which requires more of a walking pace, more space, and a supply of patience and self-control. They demand more interpretative nuances. The elite young virtuosos who are patient and do not succumb to the temptation to sacrifice musicality for sheer speed achieve this balance of showmanship and interpretation. It is extremely gratifying to test the limits of your finger dexterity. It makes for a great show. A virtuoso welcomes the challenge any day.

Not Easily Impressed

Occasionally, college students would try to show off their skills, but I ignored them. The more they tried to impress me, the more I ignored them. I'm not easily blown away. What commands my attention is when students are eager and ready to learn something new or deeper. I find students who are talented and teachable both inspiring and impressive. I am but one small talent among a hundredfold, a thousandfold, a millionfold. I've seen live performances of gifted artists on the top tier of the talent hierarchy, best in the world, and those who visited and performed in the Philippines: Glenn Gould, Gary Graffman, the Bolshoi Ballet, Andre Watts, Vladimir Ashkenazy, and Ann Schein. I saw what it took to be great at what you do. My teachers shared a level of knowledge and skill that appeared to be exclusive instruction administered to only those who study in the best conservatories and with the best teachers in the world. Talent is not enough; you must put in the time and the hard work, not only in regular practicing but also in acquiring additional skills that constitute the total package. Sight reading is one of those skills.

Sight reading became a priority and a component of my regular practice routine. Sight reading is the developed skill of reading and performing notated music that the performer has not seen before. In other words, you try to perform a piece at a reasonable tempo with all its dynamic nuances on its first reading by sight. My very first piano teacher incorporated sight reading exercises by assigning me to play works of Clementi and Kuhlau for fun, even before I was assigned specific sonatinas by said composers. It did seem like fun to be challenged to play something as though you already know it. But the exercise began when I was nine years old, part of a strict regimen to hone in sight reading skills. Then I proceeded to sight read *Mozart Sonatas*, a few Haydn *Sonatas*, Bach *Two-Part Inventions*, later *Three-Part Inventions* followed by *Preludes* and *Fugues*, and then Beethoven *Sonatas*. Imagine your practice hours not only consisting of the regular repertoire pieces of your curriculum but also playing additional music to develop sight reading skills. It's far from easy; it's a matter of going over and above.

Reading piano reductions of orchestral accompaniment for concertos subsequently ensued to develop my accompaniment

The elite young virtuosos who are patient and do not succumb to the temptation to sacrifice musicality for sheer speed achieve this balance of showmanship and interpretation.

skills. I was only thirteen when I served as an accompanist to three piano colleagues, all college piano performance majors. I learned to accompany the Mozart *Piano Concerto in D minor, K. 488*, the Beethoven *Piano Concerto in Eb Major* (*Emperor Concerto*), the Kabalevsky *Piano Concerto No. 2 in G Minor, Op. 23*, and Tchaikovsky *Piano Concerto in Bb Major*. By age sixteen, I had sight read and played the Grieg *Piano Concerto in A Minor*, the Liszt *Piano Concerto in Eb*, several Mozart *Concertos*, and the Beethoven *C Major, Bb,* and *G Major Concertos.*

Solfège singing enhances both sight reading and aural skills, and hones in your own vocal singing. It simply means you sing melodic notes using syllables of the solfège system, *Do-Re-Mi-Fa-Sol-La-Ti-Do*. *Fixed Do* solfège means *Do,* and it always refers to the actual home pitch as in C in C Major. *Re* is the second note of the scale, the actual pitch D, and so on. This approach is well suited for musicians with perfect pitch. The other system is called *moveable Do* solfège. One is said to have relative pitch if the person does not have perfect pitch. *Moveable Do* solfège is compatible with students with relative pitch. The syllable *Do* here refers to the tonal center of the key. So *Do* is the pitch C in C Major. But *Do* in another key, G Major, for example, is G, *Re* is A,

Mi is B, and so forth. *Fixed Do* is old school, conservatory style. *Moveable Do* is also rooted in Guido D'Arezzo's medieval solfège system that allows for referencing the key of the melody. *Moveable Do* has gained more popularity in American music education since the mid-1900s. Although I can adjust to the system, I am most comfortable with *Fixed Do*. *Moveable Do* was used at Queens College, but my ear-training instructors allowed me to sing *Fixed Do*. I did not want to stand out, but there was a night and day difference in my solfège singing: perfect singing on *Fixed Do*, awkward in *Moveable Do*. My classmates thought I was weird. I was grateful for the accommodation.

Memorization of all pieces was required. The review of old pieces was mandatory as one continued to expand their repertoire. It meant longer practice time. It was quite relentless. In addition, the mandatory attendance and participation in master classes and other class performances not only taught me how to critique performances objectively, but also developed mental and emotional toughness for high-stress-level events. The skill to listen for technical fluency, interpretative nuances, rhythmic precision, and tone balance was cultivated by observation, assimilation, participation, and constructive criticism. Music is a complete discipline. I was grateful for the opportunity to cultivate the skills to forge a music career.

When one submits to the complete program development and evaluation of any discipline, it is like signing a contract between two parties, such as between an educational institution and a student or between a health and fitness coach and a trainee. A comprehensive plan is created for the consumer. The consumer subscribes to the program design and delivery. Mutual trust between parties is necessary to reach the desired outcome, the final result, or the final product. All things come together. All the hard work pays off. The complete discipline makes for an impressive and satisfying achievement.

Images of Perseverance

A Marathon Man

My husband, Eli, was a runner and trained for marathons for many years until a knee problem kicked in. He would get up at 5:00 in the morning four times a week and run 5-7 miles before going to work. I asked him why he did it. The answer: "Running is exhilarating. I like the quiet time and accomplishing a goal." Eli had planned to run his first marathon before he turned 40, but he incurred an Achilles tendon injury from playing basketball with a pastor friend, Don Keehner, and a few other 20-something players at Princeton YMCA. Eli's subsequent surgery and recovery sidelined him for a few years. Eli persevered with his training, and within two years after the accident, a few months after he turned 40, Eli ran his first 26.2. But not without obstacles.

Most marathoners might say that the hardest mile might come at mile 20. Well, Eli hit the wall at the 19th mile. His legs started to go into spasms. A fellow runner, a gentleman in his 60s, stopped his run and came to Eli's rescue. The kind person coached him on what to do, encouraged him, and ran alongside him for a while. Eli called the elderly gentleman his hero. Without the help, my husband would have quit right there on mile 19. On the last mile, his legs gave up again and he fell this time. Another runner stopped and reminded him that the finish line was around the corner. The runner helped Eli up. Just around the corner was the entrance to the stadium, which Eli could not see from around the bend with all his pain and the battle within to give up. Eli called the second runner an angel. A hero and an angel came to Eli's aid, and Eli finished the race.

Eli said his first marathon introduced him to bodily pain and sensation he had not felt before the race. The mental battle was brutal. Eli thought of quitting several times, but he did not stop. He stayed on course. He remained focused and resolute to keep going. He made it to the finish line. He remembered the two men, his saviors, who cheered him on to the end. Since then, my marathon man has completed a few full marathons, half marathons, one triathlon relay, and several 10ks and 5ks. A marathoner—the fitting image of *no matter what, don't stop; take it to the end.*

> **Music is a complete discipline.**

It Wasn't Well With My Soul

The year was 1991. My family and four other families traveled for a New York mission organization. We sang at different churches in the Northeast and the Midwest to raise funding and awareness for a church that was to be planted in Princeton, New Jersey. We had just sung during the first service of a large congregation in Cincinnati, Ohio. We all returned to our seats. I quietly waited for the cue to go back and play a piano solo during the offering. Imagine me in my post-1980s look, outfitted in a satiny teal-colored dress with shoulder pads, big-hair perm, and high heels with sheer silky stockings. I was about to go up the stage when I realized that I could not get up from my seat. I was somehow stuck to the pew. I didn't know at first that my hosiery got caught on a nail right under the seat. I yanked my leg with the hopes that nobody would notice the fuss. I was already getting self-conscious. When I finally managed to free myself from the grip of the pew, I noticed the pancake-sized run on the left leg of my stockings. Here I was, about to offer a piano performance as my worship to God! But I could not, for the life of me, get over the fact that there was a run on my stockings the size of a Dunkin' Donut. Do you know what hymn arrangement I played that morning? "It Is Well With My Soul"! For sure, my soul was nowhere close to being well at that moment.

I started playing, trying to regain some kind of composure. About a quarter of the way into the piece, I noticed that something was going wrong. I was in some increasing discomfort without realizing that the horrendous pain might be coming from my fingers. I kept playing until I saw blood spewing across the white keys of the Baldwin grand piano. I felt the intense throbbing of one of my fingers. By now, the sight of the color red dominating the black-and-white landscape of the piano was about enough to send me into extreme panic. It was like being the victim in an Alfred Hitchcock movie or The Twilight Zone. For a second, I wondered if I was going to pass out. But I did not. I did not stop. I continued to play with the same determination, expressiveness, and concentration. I had to finish the piece. I had to take it to the end. After the last chord rang, I quickly exited to the back door to the right of the stage. I vaguely remember the pastor explaining to the congregation the bloody keys he saw as he was coming up to deliver his sermon. He speculated what might have happened but did not get the full story until he came backstage after he preached.

Meanwhile, an usher greeted me with a first aid kit by the time I shut the door behind me. I had a big cut on my left thumb. The pain by then was excruciating. My fingers got cleaned up, and my thumb bandaged. What just happened? How did I get injured? After the service, I went back to the pew to look for the nail. I realized then that while yanking my hosiery off the seat, my hand also caught the nail under the pew in full force. The nail cut the left corner of my thumb. Mystery solved! However, amidst the subsequent agony from the cut and the fuss around me backstage, all I could think of was that I did it. I managed to take the song to its conclusion. That was my version of endurance.

Friend and Mentor

My friend and mentor, Betty Carpenter Chapman, led a women's Bible study in her home. She started one for the women in her neighborhood. Betty was a retired elementary school principal who kept in contact with many of her elementary school parents over the years. Upon retirement, she decided to focus her energy on helping these women. There were as many as 20 ladies who came to the group study at her home two times a month. Betty, with her sister's help, picked up those who were not able to drive to her house. If someone became sick, Betty cooked and delivered meals to their homes. In addition to her Bible study, Betty also helped her church as they moved to a new facility. She was an active prayer warrior for her church, her family, her friends, her coworkers, and those who made their prayer needs known to her. She assisted in the creative efforts at her church, whether it was in decorating the space or in programming design. She contributed faithfully and lent her financial wisdom and acuity to the church. She was also an effective human-resource supporter to her congregation, always mindful of her giftedness and passion for the Lord.

During all this time, Betty was battling cancer. She delivered those meals usually two days after a chemo or radiation treatment. She taught the ladies while attached to an intravenous bag that helped her from dehydrating because of the radiation. Betty never let the stronghold of her illness confine and defeat her. She never lost that shining glow that she exuded generously to everyone. Church members continued to drop in for advice and counsel. I marveled at how consistent she was at being who she was and living her faith out despite her circumstances.

If you had Betty pray for you, you would leave with a feeling that you had been blessed by a woman who was breathing the living image of "no matter what." She did not give up. She didn't hesitate. She looked death straight in the eye and claimed her victory. She would be faithful to the end. She finished her race with grace and courage. It has been more than twenty years since her passing, but her story inspires me to this day. Her image of perseverance is inscribed in my heart.

9 | CHANGING TRAJECTORY

Why did I not stay in New York to forge a concert career that had been jump-started a long time ago by my well-intentioned family? Why did I move away from the city where I had made significant connections in the music business? Why leave a promising profession cultivated by a roster of extraordinary teachers, folks who would have helped me further my career with unquestionable dedication? Why did I get married in my early twenties when the majority of my peers opted to stay and perform in New York and chose wedded bliss much later in life?

These are questions I have been asked over the years. They have been phrased differently depending on who's asking. More often than not, it was by my New York-based music friends.

The answers were not obvious at first because not one answer was adequate. What might not have made sense to friends and family was clear to me. I began performing when I was a child. So, from the age of six to sixteen, long before I stepped into the halls of Juilliard, it felt like I already had a career. Winning the cute talent shows and piano competitions paved the way for television guest appearances and performances in concert halls. Ten years in a very young life seemed like an eternity. I was clueless at that age about the long-term implications of a prodigy's success. I later began to understand that perhaps, deep down, my reaction to a future of a performing career in my adult years was simple: *been there, done that.* I simply got tired of the rigor and wondered if I had the stamina or if I was built for the lonely lifestyle of practicing and concertizing. I was conflicted about whether or not the concert way of life would be sustainable.

The star that shone brightly had lost its steam, its brilliance. This is common among child prodigies. Only a small percentage of them survive through a successful career into adulthood, and still, a smaller group reaches international acclaim. I was becoming more self-aware of my temperament; I fretted about not wanting to become the stereotypical eccentric artist. A few of my contemporaries turned out that way, more successful than I ever was in the concert world, but at what expense? I couldn't see myself turning out alone, lonely, isolated, and out of touch with the outside world. I fought every ounce of my being to avoid eccentric tendencies and instead embrace normalcy.

As I grew older, having lived to know that life is hard and that every day brings an opportunity to decide to trust God, I began to understand the life that God has crafted for me. My musical talent has been present since I was a child. The talent was developed, and the cultivated talent never left me. It's a constant reminder of God's faithful and generous heart. I had to accept the fact that the gift I've been given had to find its way to be given away to bless others and ultimately bring honor to the Giver of Gifts. After a season of stepping out of my musical studies to consider another career, anything but music, I returned to complete a music degree with a renewed love for music. The decision was mine, not dictated by my parents, grandfather, and well-intentioned instructors. Clearly, I wanted to carve my own path for my future.

Having been separated from my parents and my brother and sisters when I was a teenager created a psychological and emotional quandary that took me years to overcome. Mama's strong presence in my young musical career nurtured my confidence in my performing abilities. She was my devoted cheerleader in all things. Her selfless companionship safely anchored me. This unselfish woman singularly protected her daughter through the unpredictably dangerous streets of Manila as we hopped from jeepney to jeepney through the crowded streets and avenues, from our home to the conservatory back to home, from lesson to lesson, and from concert to concert; quite frankly, wherever I had to be. I completely depended on her for I was not an independent person at all. I was needy and insecure, overprotected, and scared of the world. I brought along with me, upon arriving in New York City, a level of separation angst. The kind of foreboding I did not realize until I became an adult was choking me, one that I did not make time to address. I pushed it aside to handle the demands of enculturation to the new city. I made it to America! What could be better than that? No amount of homesickness for family, for Mama, or for the life I once knew could measure up to the thrill of a new adventure. However, the words of Maggie to Captain Hook in the 1991 movie *Hook* resonated loudly, "You need a mother very, very badly!"

I got married, had kids, and embraced a suburban life in Long Island, New York. Life went on. Meanwhile, my parents, sister, and brother were still in the Philippines, waiting for their immigration papers to be processed. In 1990, my parents, Papa and Mama, along with my younger sister Loida and baby brother Gedeon, were finally ready to leave the Philippines for good. After a long wait and thanks to the sponsorship of Noemi and her husband Oscar, they were set to move to Canada to join Noemi and her family. Three months before the scheduled departure, Papa had a second stroke, a year and a half from his first one. He quickly passed away, only a few months short of his 64th birthday.

Papa's passing sent me into a deep depression, something so unfamiliar, the kind that required serious therapy and medication. What started as grief counseling evolved into a painstaking journey of facing an identity crisis. Something caught up with me. There I was, so young when I left my immediate and extended family. I became an alien in a strange Western culture. I survived somehow, excelled in school, found a husband and raised our two daughters, set up a comfortable teaching studio with freelance work, and immersed ourselves in church ministry. Slowly, the therapist helped me peel the thick layers of woundedness and feelings of abandonment that laid dormant for years. I had been looking for home all this time. There was an enveloping, nagging void that wouldn't disappear after all these years. I wondered what would have been the difference had my parents, or had Mama traveled with me to the United States in the first place. Would the presence of a parent have been enough to keep me pursuing the musical goals so deeply ingrained in my soul? Would that have changed the trajectory of my life?

I mentioned earlier that I was an introspective child. Though my early life was filled with task-oriented stimulation, I delighted in times of isolation and the quiet moments that solitude presented. I liked to think and ruminate. I wrote some poetry and a few songs. Practicing the piano for hours was perfect and seemed to fall naturally into my preferred state of aloneness. However, coming to New York awakened something in me, something I couldn't have imagined so deep in my soul. The inward-looking, introverted child had to grow up quickly in New York City within a few days. The instinct of self-preservation rose from within. It was a matter of survival. All it took was the urgency to figure out how to navigate New York City all by myself. Where was Mama when I needed her the most?

Riding the subway alone would make anyone street-smart in many ways. New York attacks your delicate senses, all at once, from every corner with such an unbridled overload that you quickly develop a frenetic multitasking skill long before the word "multitasking" entered our 21st-century vocabulary. Before moving to New York, I was able to shift easily between the role of a high-achieving parochial schoolgirl and that of a composed, accomplished stage performer. However, the truth is that my academic persona was securely rooted within the high cement walls of the school, while my performing persona thrived only within the supportive environment of my close-knit family, concert halls, and television studios. I suddenly found myself in New York City, serendipitously engulfed in a way of life built on a complex system. Whether underground or on the street, I was in a city that supposedly doesn't sleep. A city, which is so much more than the iconic Central Park, made up of five boroughs, each borough teeming with enclaves of districts representing cultures of the world. A city that's truly the melting pot of the world. I welcomed the road to becoming a New Yorker, the road to independence, self-sufficiency, assertiveness, and busyness.

Since I did not have my mom to rely on, I wondered how I would survive. All of a sudden, I wasn't as confident anymore. Fear and tentativeness set in. Fear, if remained unchecked, could get out of control. Tentativeness, if not addressed, could spiral down to indecisiveness. It was such a drastic change in my normal routine and surroundings overnight. For a moment there, I thought it was all for naught if I couldn't handle being on my own. Fortunately for me, someone stepped in. I was glad she did.

Auntie

Auntie Gladys is my Uncle Mel's wife. She is Cuban. She and her mother, we called her Mima, came to the United States as refugees from Cuba. Auntie came first to New York in 1957 to look for work after the university she was attending in Havana closed down when Fidel Castro began

174

the revolution. Mima followed by herself shortly to join Auntie. Auntie managed to return to Cuba in 1959 to finish her pharmacology degree. Mima returned to Cuba with her. Auntie returned first to the States in 1961. Mima planned to join her immediately but got caught in the middle of the Bay of Pigs invasion. Mima was one of the fortunate ones to have been able to leave Cuba on short notice with nothing but a broken watch on her wrist and a grandson in tow. Her refugee story remains complicated and compelling.

Uncle and Auntie met in 1969 in New York and got married in 1971. Hardly a year into their marriage, I arrived to live with them in Queens so I could attend Juilliard. I introduced myself to her via a long letter before my arrival. It was a weird letter to send someone whom I hadn't met before. I remember writing to reassure her that I would be diligent in my studies and promise to be a good girl. That still did not seem fair to Auntie. Daddy told her and Uncle that I was coming. There was no asking from the family patriarch! What else could I have said at that time? I was not privy to the adult conversations or non-conversations that might have transpired. But what's done was done! So there I was. Reunite with a relative I had not seen in years, who now has a new wife and mother-in-law, all complete strangers to me. Mima hardly spoke English. Talk about a premise for a TV sitcom or a plain recipe for disaster. One more thing! Mima

> The instinct of self-preservation rose from within. It was a matter of survival.

and I were going to be roommates! I was shocked, to say the least. A then fifty-something Cuban American widow sharing sleeping quarters with a fresh-off-the-plane teenage Filipino! Imagine the conundrum that descended upon me, just a bit too much to handle for a spoiled brat who only a few days earlier had her own bedroom. This was not how I pictured America at all.

I did not know anything about Cuban culture. Yet I found myself thrust into a trilingual environment overnight. I understood a little Spanish because Papa spoke a version of the Spanish language. But Cuban Spanish, in America, I did not know where to begin. I thought Auntie and Mima talked Spanish faster than I had ever heard Spanish spoken. I was introduced to Auntie's extended family, including Auntie's cousin's husband, who reminded me of Ricky Ricardo in *I Love Lucy*. I found his demeanor, fair skin, dark hair, and accent all pleasantly amusing. There was also Mima's sister-in-law who played the best salsa and rumba music on the piano. I thought to myself, family gatherings would be a blast! My immediate challenge was to figure out how to communicate with Mima since she would be the first and last person I would see each day. I remember the first few weeks. Our conversations were somewhat limited to "Buenas noches" at night and "Buenos días" in the morning. That was it. I decided I better learn a lot more Spanish.

I thought I would come to New York and just have to deal with the demands of adapting to American culture, whatever I had imagined it to be, from reading the Dick and Jane and Spot stories from my childhood. I did not sign up to add another foreign language to my already-packed curriculum. But speaking Spanish became necessary. I thought I had enough problems already dealing with the New Yorker accent, daily becoming a challenge because I had to repeat "I beg your pardon" several times a day, not because I did not hear, but because I had no clue what people were saying, as though they were speaking a foreign language. Why do New Yorkers drop the "r" at the end of a word like *number*? Why do they add "r" at the end of the word, like Linda? I just wanted to hear the English accent of Walter Conkrite or whatever version Samantha used in *Bewitched*. I kept asking myself, where's America?

Life is, indeed, funny! I grew up with a father who, in addition to Tagalog and English, spoke a Spanish Creole language, *Chavacano;* a derivative of the old Spanish spoken by the Spaniards who colonized the Philippines for 300 years until the late 1800s. He tried to teach me some *Chavacano*, but I had no interest in the language. Why should I learn Spanish or any version of it? I was not moving to Spain. I was coming to America. Had I stayed through my senior year in Manila, I would have studied basic Spanish anyway in high school.

I learned to speak Spanish at home. Mima was a great conversationalist as long as it was in her native tongue. I just had to pick it up as quickly as possible, a few words and phrases at a time. I watched a few *telenovelas* with her to speed up the process. The Spanish soap opera stars were from all over the world! That's how I learned the nuances between Spanish being spoken by a Mexican or a Cuban, a

Puerto Rican, a Colombian, an Argentinian, a Venezuelan, or a Spaniard. Mima would always point out who was from which country so I could listen to the differences in the way they spoke the language. She also bought the Spanish magazine *Vanidades*. I pored over the articles to see how much Spanish I could understand in print. Mima was my first Spanish language instructor.

But it also made sense to take Spanish in high school. A foreign language was required anyway. So I did for the obvious practical reason. Pretty soon, I was able to converse fluently *en español*. I continued my study in college, three years of Spanish language. I also took two Spanish literature courses during my last year in college, more Spanish classes than I ever needed to graduate. I just fell in love with the language. All the background in the language worked to my advantage later in my graduate program. I had to have a foreign language to enter the master's program. The music graduate degree program usually accepted Italian, French, and German—the more popular foreign languages in the music discipline. However, the program accepted Spanish instead of the other languages. My deep appreciation for having learned the language peaked by the time I took the language exams as a partial fulfillment of the requirements of the Master of Arts degree. The written language examination included the translation of music-related symposium essays from Spanish to English. I breezed through it.

Learning Spanish was a piece of cake compared to the rather long list of things I still had to learn. It became clear to Auntie that I did not know much about anything except to study and play the piano. She soon realized she had to deal with a little princess. I had a maid make my bed in Manila. The maid washed and ironed my clothes. The maid set and washed the dishes. The maid swept and waxed the floors. She then polished the floors with a *bunót*, a coconut husk used by Filipinos for the job by placing a foot on the husk and using your leg to move in a such as though you were scrubbing the floor with the other leg for your balance, almost like dancing the twist.

Auntie took it upon herself to teach me to do simple chores at home. Going to the laundromat around the corner from the apartment building was a weekly ritual. It was a week's worth of dirty laundry. The amount of clothes, towels, and bed sheets to be washed and dried was unnerving. It took a good portion of the day to accomplish that. I also went grocery shopping with my Uncle and Auntie. Vacuuming the carpet and dusting the furniture, cleaning the toilet and tub, and mopping the bathroom and kitchen floors, completed the weekend chores. I thought I was going to die. More often than not, I wished I could be practicing the piano instead. However, Auntie took the time to teach me everyday chores; if you didn't call that discipline, I don't know what else it was. Additionally, Mima also taught me to sew a few dresses on the sewing machine. My greatest sewing achievement was when I helped her sew the maxi-length dress I wore for my college senior recital. I did not have my Manila couture designer this time. Using a Simplicity sewing pattern, I stitched and hemmed my own gown for my senior recital. This could not have happened in the Philippines, only in America, and all of it while keeping a tight schedule practicing the piano and pursuing a music degree. My life changed from being spoiled and privileged to being conscientious and responsible. I was on my way to learning life skills. But there was yet another skill that eluded me. I did not know how to cook.

The day I learned to boil an egg was historic. I learned to prepare breakfast, even though it was only cereal with milk, and to make my own bag lunch. Baby steps first, that's what I'd say! The sad part about the cooking gig was that here I was, a Filipino immigrant in New York City, but I did not know how to cook Filipino food. Mama did not teach me. Growing up, cooking was the last thing on my mind, though I love the traditional fare of *lumpia* and *pancit*, chicken *adobo*, any form of *guinisa* or the stir-fry variety. But while living in New York, I did not cook American hotdogs and hamburgers either or the quintessential beef stew (I saw that in *Bonanza*, a favorite US television import in the Philippines), mashed potatoes, or a variety of casseroles. How did I develop my culinary chops? I immersed myself in Cuban cooking, what else, by watching Mima cook her specialties: *flan de leche*, *frijoles negros*, *arroz con pollo*, *platanos verdes y maduros*, *bistec de palomilla*, *bistec empanizado*, *kimbombo*, *boliche*, *bacalao*, *picadillo*, *fricase de pollo*, and *yuca*. I learned to cook them all! How bizarre was that?

Auntie's and Mima's influence in my life was stronger than I even imagined. Sure, I learned the chores, but more importantly, they taught me that living in America meant developing a healthy attitude towards hard work and being grateful for the opportunities. This valuable understanding would change my future perspective. By then, Uncle, Auntie, and Mima were already naturalized citizens. They demonstrated a deep appreciation for the responsibilities and blessings that came with citizenship. Moreover, Auntie taught me that I could now make choices for myself and that I had the freedom to determine my future, not what Mama, Papa, or Daddy had decided for me. It was a novel idea. I could become whoever I want to become. I could pursue a career apart from my elders' wishes. My "de-princessization" was approaching completion. I was becoming an independent, bold, and resilient New Yorker, and I was pretty proud of it. Yet, there was still another American value I had to learn.

Work, What's That?

Growing up, my job was to practice, study, and play for the church. The concept of work was nonexistent. Earning money was from entering music competitions and playing for TV. That's what I knew about work. When I came to New York, I noticed that the majority of my high school friends made a beeline from school to go to work at McDonalds, the local drugstore or pizzeria, a car garage, or, more popularly, grocery stores like Key Food. I was completely unprepared for this. Go to work? I believed that was only for grown-ups. Nevertheless, Uncle and Auntie encouraged me to find a part-time job. They provided everything, including whatever I needed for school, bus pass money, clothes, books, and lunch. They suggested working to earn some extra pocket money. Well, attending Juilliard did not leave much room for working any part-time job. Juggling high school and Juilliard was challenging enough to be made more complicated by a part-time job. I did not look for a job while in high school. We all agreed that it was best to wait until college. I was beginning to see a life beyond just the walls of a practice room.

In the meantime, after a year and a half of adjusting to a teenage niece, Uncle and Auntie welcomed their only son, Francisco. Babysitting for my little inquisitive, bright, and bilingual cousin was a blast. He was like a baby brother. I took the time to watch PBS children TV shows with him. It was delightful to play with him and his toddler toys. I practiced speaking Spanish with Francisco but taught him English children's songs. He sang with a cute Spanish accent. Being surrounded by four adults, Francisco developed advanced language skills and later flourished in his school settings. With a seventeen-year age difference between us, Francisco and I hold the distinction of me being the oldest and him the youngest grandchildren of Daddy, with everyone else in between, an honor I hold dearly.

I applied for a student worker position at the Queens College Library in my college freshman year. I landed my first official American job with a paycheck. I worked ten hours a week at the return desk in the Main Library. Wow, I felt good about it! It was a big part of my assimilation into American society. I now had my own money and did not have to depend on an allowance from Uncle and Auntie. I loved it! Auntie advised me what to do with my first check. I went to the bank and opened a savings account. I was so proud. I did not know anything about money growing up in the Philippines. Everything was handed to me. So I was very grateful that Uncle and Auntie taught me the value of work. They said money didn't grow on trees, even though I thought that it did in America. Uncle sent money regularly to the Philippines for the needs of the family, and so did another Uncle in Canada. My siblings, cousins, and I were the beneficiaries of their generosity. I was beginning to see firsthand how hard Uncle and Auntie worked. Their work ethic was undeniable. They both got up early each morning, as early as 5:30, to get ready and catch a bus and the subway into the city. Uncle had a longer commute as he worked downtown. They both came home no earlier than 6:00 each night. I learned to appreciate even more what they had done for the extended family in Manila.

The summer before my sophomore year, a new indoor mall opened within walking distance from the house. A few anchor department stores and other small businesses were hiring part-time workers. The idea of working in a mall intrigued me. It's something different. I applied immediately at Abraham and Strauss. I got a job in the intimate apparel department 14 hours a week: two nights during the week and an 8-hour shift on Saturdays. I started this job before I declared music as my major, so I was able to handle the work hours at night. But by the end of the year, I turned around and became a music major. I continued working at the department store. Imagine balancing an 18-credit semester, practicing again every day, and a 14-hour week job. There was no time for idling. Each minute, each hour, was carefully planned and scheduled. Factor in the 10-minute walk to catch the bus and the 25-minute ride to campus; my days were long and taxing. One thing was for sure, I was in good shape from all the commuting, walking across the campus from building to building, and 14 hours a week of standing at my job post.

Subsequently, I also began teaching private piano lessons. My first students were children of Filipino immigrants from church. I taught in their homes. I arranged a two-and-a-half-hour block between my classes and the department store job to jumpstart my mobile teaching studio. Strategically selecting homes close to the mall, I slowly built my clientele from members of my local church, which had a high percentage of Asian members. I began honing my teaching skills. Soon after declaring piano performance as my major, one of my college professors recommended I teach two fairly advanced college music students who needed to take lessons. They were not performance majors in the Bachelor of Music program, but still had to prepare for jury examinations at the end of each academic year for their Bachelor of Arts degree in Music. My private teaching business was slowly growing. I juggled attending college, teaching part-time, working part-time at the mall, freelancing as an accompanist, practicing, faithfully attending a weekly young adult Bible study, and volunteering to lead a youth choir. It was all a matter of discipline. It was also a matter of embracing the opportunities to earn a living, learning the value of honest work, and trusting God that all the experiences would not be wasted as I moved towards my future.

Coming to the United States completely changed the direction of my life. I thought that I would eventually return to Manila, but I knew that I was acclimating more and more each day to Western life. I felt that New York was becoming home. What once was foreign became familiar. What used to be confusing and complicated became clear and comfortable. I began to own the promise that I can make it in this town. However, living in New York City presented its own unique set of risks and challenges. I traveled to school alone. I went to work alone. I was navigating the dangerous streets of New York in the 1970s alone. Occasionally, I thought of Mama and wished she were around during a few scary moments I had to face. If I were to make it in this city, I would have to find the courage and resolve to muck through the quagmire and escape the jeopardy that lurked in its streets.

New York Jeopardy

Why I had to leave my little safe world in Manila became a nagging question throughout my young adult life. Why be transplanted in New York City of all places? The aura of the rich musical life New York City offered did not seem to matter when you considered that the city was not a safe place to live back in the day. Reeling from the chaos of the previous decade, the New York of the 1970s confronted a grave financial crisis and an increase in drug-related murder statistics. I remember the horrible "Son of Sam" years. I remember the Times Square of that time in a not so G-rated way. Attending a Broadway show meant walking by street corners held hostage by provocatively dressed entrepreneurial women and loitering folks smoking pot, even in broad daylight. I had to carefully plan which avenues and streets to avoid any eye contact or a possible nerve-wracking encounter with what I thought to be dangerous people. I learned to be suspicious. I learned to walk at a faster pace to zigzag through parallel and intersecting avenues and streets, all of which made the city both so fascinating and so frustrating. Queens, the next borough over, was no different. One had to be careful with a heightened sense of alertness and caution coupled regularly with a stark reminder that a crime could sneak up on you at any time. My danger radar was on high alert.

Just a few months into my department store job, I fell victim to a hold-up robbery on my floor. It was 8:15 pm. The daily money drop from the cash register was on schedule. It was required that you empty the till of at least $500 to make it easier to count the rest at closing at 9:30 pm. After counting some $700 in cash, I placed the cash in an envelope, sealed it, and returned the envelope to the till. Pickup would come shortly. At least two salespersons worked in each area of the department store at night. My coworker stood right outside the boxed area enclosing the cash register. I was at the cash register, about to close it, when a young man swiftly approached me from my right side. On my left emerged my coworker with a second guy behind her, holding her with what appeared to be a concealed weapon pointed at her from within his coat pocket. I was not sure if the second man had a gun, but the way he was holding my coworker, I could only assume.

I had just turned nineteen, still being assimilated into the daunting big city life and not quite the seasoned street-smart New Yorker I should already have been. The first guy quietly asked for the envelope. It quickly dawned on me that he probably had previously scouted the different departments and determined my area was the most vulnerable. The guys were familiar with the money-drop routine. My department was next to an exit door, straight to the street and not towards the center mall area. I did not fight back. I complied, pulled back the till, pulled out the sealed envelope, and nervously handed it to him. What was I supposed to do? A possible hold-up scenario never crossed my mind. I was thinking about my coworker being held by the second guy. I was too scared to react any other way. The first guy grabbed the envelope, and just as instantly as I handed him the envelope, both disappeared in a poof, bolting out of the side door. I immediately called security. Two security employees hastily arrived and tried running after them, but to no avail. Security asked me to look through pages and pages of mug shots, but I could not do anything for them. I was too shaken up, close to hysterics. I wanted to quit my job right then and there. I also could have been fired. Neither happened. Both security personnel drove me home that night to explain to Uncle and Auntie what happened. My first direct encounter with a New York kind of jeopardy came too soon, I thought.

There were a few other incidents on New York City streets that frightened me to the core and tested my reaction to impending danger. One of those occurred two years later after the robbery. I had a 20-minute brisk walk home from the mall after work. I was usually halfway home around 9:45 pm. One of those nights, I was in more of a hurry to get home to finish an assignment. My pace was faster than usual. Within yards from the store exit, I noticed a suspicious old brown sedan slowly following me from right outside the mall area. By now, I've developed a sixth sense for any kind of looming threat.

I spotted the car while I was still walking the more-lit main streets. A few more blocks beyond and I would have had to make the usual left-right-left turns into the darker, less-lit secondary streets leading up to our house. When I was younger, the kind of troubleshooting I often engaged in was either related to piano playing or a school project. The hold-up robbery two years earlier had since made me more nervous, more wary, and extra cautious. Again, facing another precarious situation, my brain went on overdrive to figure out a possible solution. One thing was for sure, I did not want to take a chance.

I was about to take my first left turn on the street about 100 yards away when I noticed a garbage truck slowly making its collection schedule. The sedan following me stopped several yards behind me before reaching the intersection, but without making any indication that the driver was going to put the vehicle in park. The driver just stopped and idled a few yards behind me. I made a quick decision. It was now or never! I crossed the street and called out to one of the garbage men, a tall, muscular African-American in his late 30s or early 40s. I rapidly fired my suspicion and begged him to please kindly take me home in his garbage truck, whether as a passenger or inside the bin; I did not care at all. I just needed to be rescued! I was sure he didn't know what I was ranting about because I was talking a mile a minute. He paused for a few seconds, then calmly suggested that he would have to speak with his supervisor, who was in an official car close by. I followed the garbage man without hesitation. He spoke with a supervisor who was standing outside his white station wagon with a legitimate lettering of the City of New York Department of Sanitation. I already felt safe.

The supervisor was a soft-spoken gray-haired man, Caucasian. I remembered thinking that he must be Irish because although I can't recall the exact name, his name badge read "O'Something." He asked me to point to the car. I did. Both men did a quick assessment of the situation. They looked towards the direction of the car across the street as though to intentionally make the car driver and the passenger aware that we were all alerted that something fishy could be going on. Within seconds, the three of us noticed the car slowly inched up to the intersection, then immediately turned right and sped off in a flash. I wanted to cry at that moment and let out an overwrought scream, but I still had to negotiate with the supervisor, so I tried to keep my cool. After saying a few words to his employee, the elderly gentleman softly announced that he could take me home. He let the dispatcher know what he had to do in the next few minutes. I appreciated him that much more. I felt secure to be in the good hands of New York City's garbage men. I didn't expect the supervisor to go above and beyond.

The kind Mr. O'Something drove me the last few blocks to my house. He strongly advised me not to walk alone late at night anymore from work. I could not stop saying "Thank you" as I stepped out of the car. He dutifully watched as I unlocked the door. We waved goodbye and he returned to his interrupted evening. I entered the house, walked up the stairs to our second-floor dwelling, and began to cry uncontrollably as I related the entire ordeal to Uncle and Auntie.

About two months passed by. I continued walking the same route after work two nights a week without any incident. Then again one night, as I turned into the darker less-lit street, our street, but still about 4 blocks from our house, I noticed a car turned into the street with me. I did not turn around to see what kind of car. It was moving rather slowly behind me, unusual in a city where everyone rushed to wherever they were headed. I was thinking this couldn't be happening again! I couldn't be imagining things. This time, however, a garbage truck was nowhere to be found. I was all alone and vulnerable. I thought I could make a dash to the house, but it would still leave me in the open. So I quickly turned towards another house and hid behind a bush. I was not about to let whoever was following me know where I actually lived. I heard the car slowly approach, stop for a few seconds in front of the house I supposedly entered, and then slowly drive away. I patiently waited another 10 to 15 minutes. I felt stupid and scared at the same time. When I thought I was in the clear, I sprinted towards home as I frantically searched for the house key, ready to insert it into the keyhole as quickly as I could. I made it home, huffing and puffing. I cried as a sense of relief overwhelmed me. Reminiscing about the incident gave me a deeper appreciation for today's technology, especially cell phones. I could have benefited both times from having one. After the last scare, from then on, even though it pained me to spend a few dollars, I heeded the advice of Mr. O'Something not to walk alone at night anymore. I took a cab home after work two times a week. Better be safe than sorry.

Looking for Home

The eclectic nature of my experiences, both good and bad, in New York City post-Juilliard gives an overall picture of how I came into my own. It didn't happen overnight. It was the kind of growth that was borne out of my collective past. One thing is for sure, I became street smart, more independent, and more resourceful. The course I took looked both familiar and new at the same time; it had straight lines, winding roads, mountain-top highs, and deep valley lows, but it was the path I chose. Would I have done it any differently? I don't think so. Friends and family might say that the decision to leave music for a while, to leave Juilliard, then return after two years altered the course of my life. Of course, it did. But what exactly was the significant event that definitively changed the trajectory of my life? Without a doubt in my mind, it was the day I left Manila.

One thing I know, after years of therapy, is that I discovered that my identity crisis was rooted in a search for my "lost" family. From the moment I left the haven I had known all my life, my childhood home, and my family, I've been on a relentless quest to go back home. For isn't our life's journey on earth about going back home—to God, the Maker of Heaven and Earth, our Creator? Somehow, I survived. I became independent, self-sufficient, suspicious, cautious, driven, goal oriented, encouraging, reserved, and only relational to a few. Through the years, I've just been looking for my family. After college, Eli and I got married in Elmhurst, New York, at the church where we first met and rehearsed *Godspell*. We lived in Buffalo, where our older daughter, Miriam, was born two-and-a-half years later. He worked for Christ in Youth. I taught music at a Bible institute. Our journey later took us back to Long Island, where our second daughter, Melissa, was born another two-and-a-half years later. Eli worked a secular job and I was a music director at a church.

Fast forward to 1992. With our elementary-aged children, Eli and I relocated to Lawrenceville, New Jersey. We joined the team of five families, led by church growth leaders Tom and Debbie Jones, to plant a church in nearby Princeton. Eli and I became associate pastors of Princeton Community Church. It was the first time the term "worship leaders" was used to describe our roles in the worship ministry. It was, by far, the most intense, exhilarating, exhausting, relational-building, stressful, and rewarding four years our family had ever experienced. Imagine the expectations to produce and lead a weekly service in a temporary location. The team made it happen just the same. When there's a will, there's a way. In addition, I started a conservatory of music affiliated with the church. It later became the model for the community music school at the college.

Our children flourished in Princeton. We cherished the New Jersey memories because it was a lesson on gritty hard work, perseverance, staying the course, and giving our best no matter what. We moved to what I think was a tough mission field. However, the quality of family life and blessings of being in ministry that our family experienced far outweighed the challenges and sacrifices of planting a church. I thought Princeton was going to be our "forever" home. During our time there, I discovered a deeper appreciation for our nuclear family. We returned to a thriving church in 2023 to celebrate its 30th anniversary.

I'm reminded of the story of Joseph, who, through his brothers' treachery and lies, ended up in a foreign country at the lowest class of society. God honored his faith and faithfulness, restored him to a position of leadership, and later reunited him with his family. I wrote the following words as part of our family's story, beautifully framed as Christmas gifts in 2013 for each member of my extended family in Virginia, Canada, and Florida: *[Our story] is an affirmation of the goodness and faithfulness of God. Our family's journey from the Philippines to the United States and Canada is peppered with much joy and success, but also with deep pain, disappointment, and sacrifice. But as Joseph testifies in Genesis 50:20-21, "God meant it for good in order to bring about this present result, to preserve many people alive. So, therefore, do not be afraid." Our God is trustworthy.*

My siblings and I have been separated from one another

since 1970, when my sister Noemi, then eleven years old, emigrated to Canada to live with another uncle and his wife. Two years later, I moved to New York City and met my New York family. Noemi and I left the Philippines when our younger siblings were still children. I reunited with my sister Noemi in 1973. Noemi was my matron of honor when I got married in 1979. Eventually, in 1990, Loida and our brother, Gedeon, along with Mama, joined Noemi and her family in Canada. We traveled from New Jersey to Canada for a happy reunion. Following years of counseling and seeking God's restoration in my life, while at the ministry in New Jersey, I came to a realization that I finally found my "lost" family. I had been looking for so long. I found my home in Eli, Miriam, and Melissa. And now the journey back home to the Creator God continues. So, no matter what, I will not stop; I will take it to the end.

10 | A MOVIE OBSESSION

Do you have a favorite movie of all time? Maybe *It's A Wonderful Life*, *Shawshank Redemption*, *The Godfather* (is mine), *Star Wars, Amadeus*, or *Black Panther*. What I have just listed are some of my top 20 favorites. Regardless of where life took me from my prodigy years in Manila, through my studies at Juilliard and the Copland School of Music, and through my teaching years thereafter, there's one movie that has been intricately woven into the fabric of my life and my family's life journey. A childhood image embedded in my memory was the opening scene of *The Sound of Music*. I remember where I was and when it happened: at the old Odeon Theater in Manila in the late '60s. The movie started and immediately I thought, "I've never been this close to the heavens . . . so huge and majestic!" As I slowly emerged from the white landscape, the jagged peaks of towering mountains peeked through the enormous, fluffy clouds. This scene transported my imagination to a faraway place, somewhere on the other side of the world—a place I long to visit someday, even before I knew where it was. The music that accompanied the grand scenery was even more captivating. By this time, attending classical concerts about twice a month was already part of my routine. I had already played with an orchestra. My trained ear was already capable of identifying the different families of instruments. There was no mistaking the French horn call at the beginning of the overture, beckoning the listener to prepare for the magical story about to unfold, in *deluxe* vision.

It was a hot ticket, only being shown in an exclusive 8-week run in Manila. Papa took Noemi, Loida, and me, his three girls, on a date to the cinema. It was standing room only. Yes, we stood during the entire movie, from beginning to end. For the three young girls, that was a huge commitment for our little legs and feet. I remember there was an intermission, the perfunctory ritual to change the reels of the movie. The screen just about filled my panoramic vision. I could see the silhouettes of people of different sizes and shapes filling the bottom of the big tube with my little sisters' tiny heads at the bottom of the frame. I remember my legs got very tired. I remember Papa picking us up, one at a time, so that each of us could have a chance to see the movie from a higher level and, more importantly, to relieve our tired little feet. He held Loida, the littlest, most of the time.

Needless to say, we all grew up with an affinity for the movie. We all agree today that the day remains a favorite remembrance of our father. *The Sound of Music* became monumental worldwide before it even arrived in Asia. Yes, the grandeur of the cinematic picture is etched in my mind, but the image of the person who made it happen is forever engraved in my heart.

But there is more to *The Sound of Music*.

By 1970, the musical reached global success. I was attending an all-girl Catholic school, so one can only imagine what the movie meant to young impressionable Catholic girls. Every preteen and teenage girl in my school wanted to be Maria. The singer and the convent postulant, Maria, was about to take vows of chastity, poverty, and obedience. I wanted to become a nun like Sister Yolanda: a young, kind, gentle, and nurturing advisor from ICAM. And I had a crush on the Captain. It didn't matter that he was an older man already with seven children.

Watching a musical was the furthest thing from my mind. But there was something about the music and lyrics in *The Sound of Music*. Each song caught the attention of my developing ear for melody, harmony, and orchestration. The orchestral scoring was perfect for the movie scenes. Our glee club sang "Edelweiss," and fledging piano players tackled "Do-Re-Mi" on the keys. For a drama competition in seventh grade and inspired by the story of survival of the Von Trapp family, I wrote and directed a short play, roughly based on *The Sound of Music* story but without music. Though our team did not win, the experience whetted my appetite for plays and musicals. By my high school freshman year, I played the lead role in a musical, *Bernadette*, based on the life of St. Bernadette of Lourdes. Playing the role of a Saint, such as St. Bernadette, St. Teresa of Avila, St. Joan of Arc, or St. Clare of Assisi, was a coveted role in Catholic school musical productions.

The Sound of Music became a staple entertainment in our family. The film equally captured the imagination and devotion of my daughters. The videotape version is probably the most worn-out tape in our archaic collection. Not only did the girls know all the songs, they could also recite the entire screenplay from memory. By the time my daughters were five years and three years of age, they were singing at family gatherings. The thread of the movie continued to be woven into our family life over the years. After the girls' full immersion into *The Sound of Music* movie, another film, *Annie*, followed suit. The girls became immediate fans of the little orphan girl and her dog, Sandy. The song "Tomorrow" became the girls' new showstopper song. On Melissa's seventh birthday, we took her and her older sister, Miriam, and a few of Melissa's friends to a community production of *Annie* in Long Island. It was their first theater attendance.

Since then, our daughters have consumed every movie musical from *Mary Poppins* to *Bedknobs and Broomsticks*, from *The Wizard of Oz* to *Oliver*, from the 1991 *Beauty and the Beast* to every Disney film since. In 1994, my husband and I formally introduced them to Broadway. We wanted to celebrate Melissa's first double-digit birthday in a special way. My husband, Miriam, and I surprised her with a late morning train ride from Princeton to Penn Station to attend a matinee performance of the smash hit *Les Misérables*. Little did we know the seed that was about to be planted in our children's psyche on that train ride to the city. On that day, Miriam and Melissa discovered their common love of Broadway musicals.

Our family joyfully embarked together on this musical journey. Our girls love to sing, that was quite clear, and not just simple pop songs but full-length show tunes. Melissa would try to sing "Castle on a Cloud," and of course, to our biased ears, she sounded like the waif Cosette. Miriam's choice was "On My Own," which she would belt out with all her might. Their dad or I would accompany them at the piano. Then *Miss Saigon* followed next. My husband and I worried about the adult-themed content of *Miss Saigon*. It was not only about a historical time in our nation's foreign involvement in Vietnam but also about prostitution in a war-torn city. It was no secret to family and friends that both our girls' dream role was to play Kim, Miss Saigon herself, a lady of the night. But then again this was the same dream role of every young aspiring Asian female singer in the early 90s. The role model here was not necessarily the fictional Miss Saigon, but instead, Lea Salonga, the Filipino singer who won the coveted inaugural role of Miss Saigon when she was only eighteen years old. Ms. Salonga's voice is classic, pure, and intimate, and she is a good role model of a singer for our girls. So we did not find our daughters' dream disturbing at all. We took them to see *Miss Saigon* the following year. Since our family celebrated special occasions by going to a Broadway show, the list of musicals that we have attended together started to grow: *Aida*, *Crazy for You*, *Phantom of the Opera*, *Beauty and the Beast*, *Tarzan*, and *Wicked*. Years later, when the girls had become young ladies, they flew to New York to watch shows like *The Lion King*, *Rent*, *Dirty Rotten Scoundrels*, *Next to Normal*, and *Mary Poppins*, among others.

The fascination with musicals can be directly traced back to *The Sound of Music*, the one that started it all. The film continued to reappear in our lives in newer versions, as though reminding us that the story of Maria and her family was our first true love. In her junior year of high school, Melissa auditioned for Lake Brantley High School's production of, you guessed it, *The Sound of Music*. Melissa had no prior experience in theater outside of a few lead roles in Christmas or spring church plays back at Princeton and a stint with Miriam in the children's choir of a local community production of *Joseph and the Amazing Technicolor Dream Coat*. Melissa knew it was a long shot. But she landed the role of one of the nuns, the Von Trapp maid, and was a finalist at the farewell concert. The rehearsal schedule was demanding, but she was determined to be a part of the production. Melissa knew she had to balance her artistic pursuit with her honors classes, as well as the time-consuming process of applying to colleges. Her best friend, Kelly, won the role of the Reverend Mother. Melissa was beyond ecstatic.

The Sound of Music effect continues. Melissa was about to complete her freshman year at the University of Florida. She had declared a double major: fine arts in piano performance and history. She announced that she had applied and had received a scholarship for a summer study abroad in Salzburg, Austria. I was ambivalent. The professors of the study abroad program, those of UF and of Salzburg College, proved trustworthy. All of the students going were musicians, the really serious kind. Melissa was going to have the chance to study Mozart with teachers who live and breathe Mozart. If she was going to study Mozart, what better and more idyllic location than Salzburg, the birthplace of Wolfgang Amadeus. And let us not forget, Salzburg was also the birthplace of *The Sound of Music*.

Melissa's stories of walking the streets of Salzburg, traipsing on the banks of the Salzach River or wandering the Mirabell Gardens, The Fortress, Altstadt, Schönbrunn Palace, Mozart's birthplace, St. Florian Monastery, and the Bruckner organ were all captured in beautiful photo mementos. She practiced for hours, took piano lessons, attended classes and concerts, made strudels, took the bus to school, and embraced the everyday life in Austria. She studied the *Mozart Piano Sonata in A minor, K. 310*, and the first movement of the *Mozart C Major Piano Concerto* and immersed herself in music history studies. Melissa acclimated to the sweet supper of strudel, bread, and cheese at Frau Repp's home. She sang and danced "I Am Sixteen" inside the notorious gazebo and visited the landmarks that made *The Sound of Music* iconic. Whimsical weekend escapades to Vienna took the group to Beethoven's Pasqualatihaus, a concert by the Vienna Boys' Choir, a performance of Puccini's Tosca at the Vienna State Opera, and a concert by Alfred Brendel at the Konzerthaus. Melissa also took a sobering tour of Dachau in Munich. I tried to walk through all of them in my mind as Melissa was describing her experiences in detail, as though I had also gone to that part of the world. Yes, there are many places of interest for a music geek like me, but really, my dream is to run up the hill like Maria did in the movie; sooner, while I can still semi-run. Melissa lived that dream.

Speaking of Munich, I had an opportunity to study in Munich as part of my graduate program, but I turned it down. I could not leave the babies who were respectively only three years old and one year old then. To have studied in Germany and to have visited Salzburg both would have been fantastic. Munich and Salzburg are dream destinations for a classic art musician. So I wonder now, who's the one living vicariously through her daughter?

After a long haul, I received my Doctorate of Education from Nova Southeastern University. Loved ones from Virginia, New York, Florida, and Ontario, Canada, watched me walk at commencement. A trip to Canada seemed quite the fitting, relaxing follow-up to my accomplishment. My sister, Noemi, invited the sisters for a girls-only trip to Toronto. Since then, we found ourselves trying to make up for lost time. To show our appreciation for each other, we occasionally indulge in treating one another. We are not wealthy by all means, so lavishing on one another may be perceived as being extravagant and ostentatious. But the joy of giving to another far outweighs the cost of our little acts of extravagance. Besides, to ease our guilt feelings, we do prepare and plan for the occasional splurge.

When the extended family comes to Florida, it becomes my husband's and my pleasure to host them. We save money to be able to purchase Disney tickets, in addition to complimentary tickets we could scrounge from friends or family. We also save money to be able to take the family to a fun restaurant, like Germany's Biergarten at Epcot, complete with the fireworks finale at the park's closing time. Another favorite destination is Sanaa in Kidani Village or Boma at the Animal Kingdom Lodge. Loida and Gedeon splurge on us when we visit Washington, DC. A special treat one time was dining at a favorite restaurant of the late President George H. W. Bush, Peking Gourmet Inn, in Falls Church. Gedeon lavishes on the sisters with a pampered treatment at the Red Door Spa of Elizabeth Arden. A trip to the nation's capital might also mean a day trip to New York City. On one of those trips during the Christmas season, Loida purchased tickets to watch the Radio City Music Hall Christmas show. We don't go on cruises or expensive destination vacations. We just want to be together where each one lives. We want to hang out, make up for lost time, eat our home-cooked specialties, tell stories of our childhood until the wee hours of the next morning, and have our two-hour-long prayer sessions. The nieces and nephews get a kick out of the prayer time because each child gets prayed over, whether they are there or not, whether they are just eleven years old or thirty years old.

Noemi would take her turn in Canada. She had hoped that the three sisters could catch a Shakespeare play one summer in Stratford, Ontario. That plan was postponed to another time when she discovered that *The Sound of Music* was coming to Toronto for a limited run. She bought tickets for a matinee performance on a Saturday afternoon. I flew into Detroit on a Thursday. The three sisters drove the next day to visit Noemi's daughter and her family at Midland. We talked so much in the car that we didn't even notice the five-hour drive it took us to get to her daughter's house. I got to meet my two great nephews, Malcolm and Josiah. We stayed at a hotel that evening, a splurge when we could have stayed at my niece's. We spent the night reminiscing about our younger life in the Philippines and our adult life in various cities in North America. But we couldn't wait until the next day.

We drove the one-and-a-half-hour ride to Toronto. We ate lunch at a New York-style restaurant that featured high-end delicatessen sandwiches, borscht soup, and matzo ball soup. That was a blast. Then, it was time for the show. The moment of truth had arrived; here we were, watching the live theater production of *The Sound of Music,* together again after four decades since we saw the movie. Noemi admitted that she had long awaited to see *The Sound of Music* musical with the sisters. She, too, had held onto the memory in her heart, the movie date with Papa when we were kids. It had been her dream to recreate a similar experience with all three sisters together. We were riveted by the performances. From the beginning to the end of the show, each song was epic, each character larger than life. We marveled at the ability of theater magic to transport us to our childhood past. At the very end, as the Von Trapp family climbed the Alps (which, thanks to modern set design technology was one of the most fantastic contraptions I had ever seen), we heaved a big sigh of relief, a little misty-eyed

Life is but a series of mountains to scale, streams to cross, and rainbows to pursue to reach our dreams.

and unanimously decided that Salzburg makes our bucket list for a girls-only road trip. By the way, the song "Climb Every Mountain" is still my favorite. Life is but a series of mountains to scale, streams to cross, and rainbows to pursue to reach our dreams. For as long as there is life, every breath is an opportunity to continue, to take the journey to the end, no matter what.

11 | FORMING GOOD HABITS

I am not one to hand out easy tips to be successful in anything. I would not dare be presumptuous. The lessons I learned came from simple hard work, putting in the time, and following a prescriptive set of rules and procedures that quickly became habits—good habits. It's what worked for me. Maybe, just maybe, it might work for another person. So for the sake of a reader who desires some helpful tips, this section is for you. The examples come from different perspectives, music, spiritual disciplines, study, health, exercise, and sports. However, the principles are the same and can be applied to various situations. If you would like to get on the path of practicing discipline, I hope the following might spark an interest. If you are already taking a similar road, then your decision might be affirmed by the following words. Breaking a bad habit takes more work, but forming a good habit and replacing the bad habit with the good habit is easier. Learning good habits early in life proves beneficial later on, but it is never too late to acquire them. One has to give it a try. Good habits bear good fruit and are more sustainable for a better and more productive life.

1. **Create an Environment to Practice Discipline**.

It is imperative that if you want to produce good results, you have to have the right equipment and the right location. A good, well-tuned instrument is non-negotiable. It will inspire you each time you play it. A bad instrument or any form of subpar substitute will annoy and zap every ounce of resolve in you. It is the same with sports equipment. You must have a tennis racket with a weight, grip size, and balance that matches your needs. Likewise, a well-lit and comfortable room conducive to practicing for long hours will encourage you to spend hours in the room. The environment will help you focus instead of causing you to get distracted. If you have a writing project, this will be most significant. Claim the environment. Circumstances may not be ideal, so if it happens to be a shared room, set up a schedule that includes time that belongs to you and time that belongs to a family member or roommate. Ask everyone concerned to embrace the set schedule. If the gym is not an option, create a space in the garage or in your bedroom to do your stretches and endurance building. If the library is not an option, try your back porch or a nearby park or garden. For good study or homework habits, do not multitask and add watching Netflix or YouTube to the mix. Give your task its full attention, but identify the environment that will help you focus on the task.

I marvel at how the coffee enterprise Starbucks created a workplace environment for the millennial generation. Other similar businesses followed suit. I walked into one local coffee shop one night and observed how every single seat was occupied, each customer with a laptop, either doing research, reading, or conducting business. The younger folks appeared to have claimed the space created specifically for them, the target group, with the guarantee of free WIFI and at your own expense, unlimited access to caffeinated drinks.

Because I learned one specific study habit does not mean another way is wrong. I did not try the laptop in a coffee shop method because I am from an older generation. I learned study habits that fostered complete silence and focus. Today's modern establishments guarantee multiple stimuli from all directions. When I am writing a paper, I need complete silence. I don't even listen to a playlist, not even Mozart or Maverick City. There is no *polonaise* in the background, or the calmer Andrew Peterson's "Is He Worthy" ringing in my ear. Music without words distracts me as it is. My problem is that I will start analyzing the form of the music. I hear every chord and nuance in the performance, so I will stop what I'm doing and listen. I will not stay true to the task. Music with words is worse. I analyze the phrase structure. I look for the rhyme, the metaphors, and whether the praise song is theologically sound or not. It's not fun to be distracted by music. Good habits were formed when I was a child. To focus on learning something new, like playing the piano, I had to learn to be alone with my piano in a room where distractions had been eliminated. The environment was intentionally created to delve into a focused practice routine. Back in the day, to study for an exam or to write a paper, I went to the library, where silence was enforced. Find the best environment that would best support you in giving your full attention to your work. You will become more productive and efficient when your surroundings support your goals.

2. Create a Plan and Schedule, and Stick to It.

Begin by planning a simple schedule. Set the goal in small increments at a time. Sterner gives sound advice, "Break down the overall goal into small sections that can be achieved with a comfortable amount of concentration . . . [this] gives you repeatable success."[1] An example I want to share is how to achieve some modest success in what so many start with good intentions but miserably fail more often than not—that is, reading the Bible in a year. You will not get anywhere in your Bible reading endeavor unless you follow a simple reading plan with realistic goals. First of all, the random opening of the Bible and letting the Spirit lead you to a passage is not going to work. A few years back, I contributed a chapter and a half to a collaborative book called *Rooted in Christ*. The following advice is part of what I have written.

> Start with a short-term plan . . . The goal is to successfully follow a simple schedule instead of aiming to read the Bible in its entirety in one year . . . Commit to reading a chapter a day . . . After reading one chapter, look for something new that you glean from reading the passage that day. It could be a verse or two. Meditate on those words. Underline or highlight the verse, and write down your thoughts and the date when you read that passage. Sometime in the future, when you reread the

same chapter, you may be able to recall the thoughts, feelings, and circumstances surrounding that first reading. You may then recognize how God has been at work in your life.

Start with the Book of Psalms. The Psalms are a collection of Hebrew poetry, many written by King David, some by the master musicians in the Temple, and some by Moses and King Solomon. The Psalms teach us how to worship, delight in God's Word, live our lives, view God, and how to pray. It will teach you how to cry to God in times of failure or distress, how to be still, and how to rejoice in His presence . . .

Next, read the Book of Proverbs. This book provides guidelines for godly living: what to stay away from, what to avoid, what to strive for, and what is common sense living. You will find good advice for handling your tongue, hands, feet, ears, and money . . .

After Proverbs, go to the Gospel of John. The book affirms the deity of Jesus Christ and also chronicles His life, ministry, death, and resurrection . . . Then, go back to Genesis. Go all the way back to the beginning and see how our relationship with God began. Be encouraged that God had you in mind from the very beginning of time . . . Learn about relationships (both good and bad) between God and His creation, God and man, and between one man and another. Grab ahold of God's sovereignty, love, providence, and faithfulness.[2]

If it is a daily routine of exercise you want to conquer,

start with a goal you can reach. You can measure the goal in minutes, in steps, or in miles. The more realistic goal for me was 30 minutes in the beginning—whatever I accomplished within that period of time. The 30 minutes became 45 minutes, then an hour. The best time for me is in the morning. We live in a warm place, so getting up at 6:00 am works well into my schedule. If the exercise is measured in steps, log in 10,000 steps a day. For music practice, well, it depends on how advanced you are. Teachers hand out guidelines and practice logs. Carving out the time will be the challenge because distractions abound. An urgent matter will deviate your attention, but you can't be flippant about practice time. Doing the time is key to your success. If you are motivated enough to be the best you can be on an instrument, create a plan and schedule, and stick to it. You will be on your way to establishing a good habit that will reap dividends in the future.

3. Take Small Breaks.

Part of following a planned schedule is break time—to take a few minutes and walk away from the task. Literally, yes, walk and do your steps. Take a small break. Take your eyes off the computer for a few minutes. Take your hands off the instrument. Rest your arms, hands, and fingers. Do shoulder stretches and neck rolls. Close your eyes and take a power nap to snap you back to mental alertness. Rest your mind. In any exercise routine, the duration of rest is pivotal to the success of the workout. The mind and body, engaged in a practice mode, need a brief respite here and there. It is necessary to stop and recharge. Any repeated task will use the same muscles and can result in fatigue. Inserting periods of rest or silence into a rigid schedule of hard work will bring relief and refreshment to your tired mind and body.

When I was planning out my writing schedule for this book project, I wanted to see how the schedule was going to look in the long term. Which days would I write? How many hours a day? I wondered how I might keep it going within reason, with a healthy mindset, without suffering through the tedious long hours of thinking, researching, and typing. Coincidentally, we received a Christmas gift from the parents of our son-in-law. I discovered how to effectively utilize their gift of two beautiful sandglass timers to balance work and rest. One timer with black sand runs for 30 minutes, and the other smaller hourglass with white sand runs for 5 minutes. Sure, I could have easily set up alarms on my smartphone, but why would I want to ignore the aesthetics of an ancient practice of measuring the passage of time? An hourglass is more exotic and connects me to the past. Yes, a bit archaic, but appropriate. The project focused on valuable lessons of good habits from the foundational practices of my past. So, symbolically, I used the hourglass, an old-fashioned "throwback" device to measure time. Stolen brief moments of reflection crept in various split seconds of my time here and there when I paused to check what I had just typed. I caught myself mesmerized by the downward flow of fine granular sand. I thought of a timeless truth. The daily introduction of an old TV soap opera, *Days of Our Lives* (I watched soap operas but not this one), rings true, "Like sand through the hourglass, so are the days of our lives." By using the sand glasses, I noticed that my writing productivity increased because of the break I took intermittently to walk away and do my steps. Who knew?

Leonardo da Vinci gave good advice: "Every now and then go away, have a little relaxation, for when you come back to your work your judgment will be surer. Go some distance away because then the work appears smaller and more if it can be taken in at a glance and a lack of harmony and proportion is more readily seen."[3] This is good advice for any artist or medium. On the other side of resting and taking a break is the promise of the capacity for more productivity. The Roman poet Ovid framed it this way: "Take rest; a field that has rested gives a bountiful crop."[4] Brief periods of rest re-energize both the body and spirit. The musical rest is the symbol that represents the moment of silence we hear between notes or musical phrases. The rest breathes in rhythmic interest and balances the symphony of sounds. Without the rest, there is no music, for music is made up of a series of sounds and silences. It is the combination of the notes and rests that creates the rhythmic flow of a musical piece. In the same manner, taking small breaks or resting is part of nature's cycle and gives balance to the rhythm of life. Take small breaks from your task or practice. It will refresh you to do better work.

4. Maximize the Use of Your Time.

When one submits to a discipline, time is golden. To stay healthy, it is recommended that an adult get at least 7-8 hours of sleep. This will keep you functioning at your best during your waking hours. Another 6-8 hours is devoted to your job or to attending school, doing homework, and studying. Then there remains another third of 24 hours to utilize. Realistically, when I used to devote 4-6 hours to practicing, within that last third of available time, I didn't have much time to do other things. But today's technology makes it difficult to ignore the distractions, released like arrows, that come our way during our waking hours. We are now connected to the world. I used to not think about what may transpire in the lives of my childhood friends on the other side of the world, but Facebook changed all that. The notification alert on our smartphone brings up a constant update on news in our community and around the globe or text messages from a friend. Compounding that with Instagram, YouTube, TikTok, and interactive live-streaming services, we find ourselves constantly clicking buttons. Productivity is beginning to be more elusive. Self-control has now become a sought-after commodity. The call to maximize the use of your time has now become more and more integral in the pursuit of discipline. How can you maximize your time practicing your instrument or engaging in a discipline-driven task?

I recall an incident during our time in New Jersey and at Princeton Community Church where my habits were tested. Both of our daughters were in middle school. I was the typical mom who drove a van and rotated in carpooling duties, and I was also teaching part-time. Life was as busy as it was. I remember getting a call to be a rehearsal accompanist for the Trenton Opera. I was given one week to learn the accompaniment to an entire *verismo* style of opera. The music was not as easy to sight read, but since I was also a freelance musician, I accepted the gig, of course! Given the limited time to learn the music, I readjusted my weekly schedule. After all, in addition to being a working mom, there were chores to complete and appointments to keep during the day before I taught most afternoons into the evening. Life did not stop because I had to practice for a gig. After the morning commotion of getting the kids ready and sent off to school, like clockwork, I practiced the orchestral score reduction from 9:00 am to 1:00 pm with a 30-minute lunch break. Every day, Monday through Friday, I carved a block of time to prepare for rehearsals. The week was intense. I assessed the overall music. I had to learn to play an entire score like I've been playing it all my

Taking small breaks or resting is part of nature's cycle and gives balance to the rhythm of life.

life! I divided the music into sections: which arias were the most difficult and which were fairly easy to read. While I was learning new music each day, I had to polish up what I had learned the day before. It was extreme learning and practicing like I've never done before.

It was again one of those moments when I retrieved learned skills from my arsenal of the past. The familiarity of a rigorous routine was effortlessly accessed. Discipline swiftly returned like it never said goodbye. I had to troubleshoot the big picture so that each hour was utilized wisely. I was determined to maximize the use of the four hours of practice each morning because I was even more determined not to allow my work to creep into precious family time that was left of the day. The motivating factor for me to manage time wisely has always been to make time for people and things I deem more important. Whether it's being on time for the kids' concerts, picking them up from school, or not wasting time to meet a deadline, I tried to maximize the use of time to free up more time for things that matter more. That is the best stewardship of time.

5. Correct the Mistakes.

Keep fine-tuning the process to reach your goal. In pursuing a good habit, whether practicing an instrument, exercising, or dieting, mistakes happen all the time. Neglecting to fix them might set you up for failure subsequently. For example, when you are on a path to dieting or healthy eating, it is important to evaluate that you are eating correctly. It makes sense to make adjustments to your diet plan if you find out that you might be missing out on essential nutrients to the body. What is paramount to any diet regimen is that you get the benefits of balanced nutrition from a variety of food sources, not just eating the same food you like best over and over. If you are not getting enough protein from a plant-based diet, what kind of corrections could you make to succeed in this plan? What kind of supplements should you take so your body does not get depleted of necessary nutrients, minerals, and vitamins? A constant evaluation of the process also will help you see the overall results and make revisions or improvements to your diet.

When I asked parents of younger piano students to describe their children's practice time, they would say that the kids practiced all the time. When further prodded, they related that upon careful listening, they noticed that the students practiced the same thing over and over again and that the children would practice the parts they liked best and played best. An undiscerning parent might conclude then that their children practice all the time. Unfortunately, the truth was that the sections that required more work were ignored, and the passages that needed improvement were left unchecked or glossed over. Without the painstaking practice of carefully correcting the mistakes, with a slower practice tempo, perhaps, or by a deliberate finger exercise on the passage, the students returned to their next lesson playing the same mistakes on the same weak spots. Take care of the problem(s) once and for all, correct the mistakes, and then enjoy the much-improved music. Don't expect to wing it.

You develop and submit good habits because discipline builds character. Put in the work and use your time wisely. If you have an hour, make that hour count. In practicing piano, use that hour to work on the trouble spots repetitively but with direction and intentionality to make corrections. Don't keep playing the piece from beginning to end. Go to the source of the problem. Do not fluff your practice. Do not avoid the parts that are the hardest to conquer. Spend time in that wilderness. Face the difficult sections with a plan to eliminate the errors. Do not take the easy way out. Do the time. Taking shortcuts is the bane of discipline.

Occasionally, it may be impossible to eliminate distractions. Some are simply unavoidable or may even be out of your control. The beauty of the practice discipline is that it prepares you for the inevitable. It sharpens your response mechanisms and enables you to troubleshoot on the spot if you do the work ahead of time. Discipline develops troubleshooting acumen. You are always on the edge during a live performance, so to have resilience is a virtue. Surprisingly, the process of correcting the errors during practice, doing the repetitions to master the corrected passages, and putting in the time will help you respond positively to unforeseen glitches that may occur during a performance. Forget taking the easy road. Have patience and endurance. Do not seek relief. Do the hard work. It is what builds character and what enables you to improvise should a disaster happen.

Mistakes happen. A performer cannot completely avoid missteps. If mistakes are inevitable, the goal is to minimize them and to respond with a sense of resolve, not to fall apart, not to give up, but instead, take it to the end. Preparation and discipline develop a determination in you to muck through the diverted attention or distraction. In sports, doing the hard time of repetitive practicing gives you a better

Preparation and discipline develop a determination in you to muck through the diverted attention or distraction.

shot at making those wild, awkward three-point-line shots in basketball, the Hail Mary passes in football, and the stolen bases in baseball. In concerts, when you go into your performance feeling that you have meticulously prepared as best you can, it builds tenacity, a kind of well-informed "no matter what happens" attitude that helps you forge ahead to the end.

12 | REDISCOVERING DISCIPLINE

When you live past the half-century mark, you look at life from a combination of retrospect, introspection, and hope. You reflect on your life experiences: the boldness of your idealistic youth, your academic achievements or shortcomings, the blessings that came from good decisions, and the consequences of poor choices. You think about the unanswered questions, the "what-ifs" that occasionally haunt you, the joy derived from stable and nurturing relationships, the uncertainty surrounding those that challenged your patience, and the sadness over those that ended. You look back, and sometimes, you realize there is not much to say except, "Thank you, God." A heart of gratitude is the only proper response to Him who has taken you through each season of life, through each battle of your growing-up years, through each success and disappointment, the many turns and detours you've taken, both the familiar paths and the roads less traveled.

And the list goes on: for missed opportunities, a series of regrets, a recurring pain that won't go away, unfulfilled dreams, or losing your loved ones by physical death, divorce, or separation. You thank God for all these things, as well. For the simple joy of having a family, having raised your children, the unexpected friendship graciously extended by your grown children, the palpitating hope for future generations, the unhurried journey of growing old with someone you deeply love, and the extra blessings of an extended family, you thank God for all these things. For the humbling privilege of making a difference in your students' lives, the providential opportunity to engage your mind, heart, and soul in ministry, and the distinct honor of trying to please God and take delight in Him, you thank God for all these things. Every experience, good and bad, is a gift that can be unwrapped to reveal more of God's generous heart and His capacity to love beyond measure.

> Every experience, good and bad, is a gift that can be unwrapped to reveal more of God's generous heart and His capacity to love beyond measure.

Life follows a different tempo in every season. When I was a younger musician, I played everything faster. *Allegro* or *vivace* seemed to be my preferred tempo for every piece. The swifter, the better! I performed Bach, Mozart, Beethoven, and Chopin in the fast lane in quest of technical brilliance and fluency. But as I got older, a more mature musicality set in. Taking time to enjoy the composition and relishing the sonority and resonance began to replace the frenetic drive of my younger years. And as I started to take time to relish, to pause, I began to remember and pay attention. As I got older, a deliberate decision now to slow down the tempo of each piece I play is but the perfect partner to accompany the natural slowing

Life follows a different tempo in every season.

down of the pace of life. When one begins to slow down, one begins to appreciate more and to thank more. A grateful heart certainly becomes a delightful treasure to a person who is growing older.

The opportunity to write on a topic that not only gives a perspective of my life as a child prodigy but imparts some helpful tips, especially for students who want to fully develop their God-given talent, was challenging from the onset. The plan all along was to write something not too academic but a topic with some practical applications. It's an opportunity to give a small glimpse not only into the life of an aspiring musician but also of a storied music conservatory that produced the best artists worldwide. So, after much reflection on what exactly would be the recurring theme or guiding principle that would weave into the different aspects of life, from family upbringing, educational experiences, career goals, personal journey, and implications on living life, it all made sense to write about the practice of discipline and good habits. It was an "Aha" moment.

How do you write about discipline without practicing what you preach, so to speak? How do you propose to an audience to subscribe to a lifestyle without considering living its tenets or some form of its principles for the duration of the project? It did not make sense to me to expound on such a topic without practicing it firsthand, for I am a practical person. I felt that the credibility factor was necessary. So, as I started narrowing down the focus of the writing, the parts came together like pieces to a puzzle. I identified three areas in my life where I would exercise a measure of discipline simultaneously as I would be writing away about discipline and good habits.

First, I started a daily routine of practicing the piano again, at least three hours a day, five days a week. It took only a few weeks to get back to what I felt would be a sustainable schedule. It felt good! The secret weapon of drills and exercises came in handy as I retrieved exercises from my memory vault to shape up the fingers, the hands, the arms, and the shoulders. In addition, I set up a nightly routine to walk up to the piano and play one song before going to bed. I did the same thing each morning. Usually, it was a piece I was trying to memorize. The sixty-repetition rule was nearly achieved in a month and maybe more in two. There was no doubt that there was constant live music at home. The saying "practice what you preach" has never been more present than it was during this writing project. I lined up a list of repertoire, some performed from long ago, a few recently learned, Beethoven, Chopin, more Chopin, Mendelssohn, and Schumann. It has been refreshing to devote myself again to the practice routine. It's familiar, stimulating, and rewarding. To have achieved good results because of a dedicated practice schedule was a constant reminder of and cause for gratitude for the gift I have received. Practicing became my new hobby.

But why would I be practicing hard today anyway? What

about other hobbies? Some spend a great deal of time working out in the gym or running for miles. Some join book clubs and community choirs. Some pick up painting or video gaming. Back in New Jersey, my friend Lisa introduced me to her card-stamping hobby. Over the years, her hobby became a small arts and crafts business for her. I loved stamping. I remember that stamping with Lisa, her children, and mine was one of the most enjoyable times I've ever experienced. I should get back into it. I also love to travel. My older daughter, Miriam, works hard to earn a living but also loves to travel the world with her friends. They plan each trip meticulously to ensure the trip is worthwhile. They go off the beaten path, away from the major tourist attractions. Their adventurous spirit has taken them to Europe, North Africa, the Canadian Rockies, national parks, and the Caribbean islands. I hope to travel more and check off the items on my bucket list. But these days, my hobby is simple. It is to play the piano again and to practice.

Ironically, what began as a necessity in order to compete and perform today has become a pleasurable pastime. At Johnson University, much of how I taught, whether music theory or music history, was rooted in performance repertoire. I demonstrated each music period by playing the works of the great masters, solo and orchestral reductions, on the piano. I practiced to keep in shape and to be performance-ready for my lectures. As I found myself practicing more and more over the last few years, I thought of putting together a repertoire for a benefit concert. I still have the technique. Why not? I found a reason to get back on the road of discipline.

Secondly, because of a hereditary predisposition towards several chronic diseases, it did not come as a surprise that I began dealing with one particular condition when I was in my mid-thirties. My siblings and I began to compare our varying ailments, most of which we concluded we inherited from our parents but seemed to have been distributed among us. What a sister has, I don't. What I have, perhaps another sibling doesn't. The list is long. So is the list of prescriptions. To proactively address my health problem became a personal goal and priority. My younger daughter, Melissa, in her sweetest effort to provide a solution, strongly suggested a radical change in my eating habits. She embarked on a mission to introduce me to something different by asking me on a date to a particular kind of restaurant. She asked me to be open-minded. She dutifully explained that it's kind of a hippie joint, not to be confused with the word *hipster*. I reminded her of the year I was born, certainly not yesterday, and that I know what a hippie is! Following the scrumptious different kind of meal and a green smoothie for dessert, she drove me to the movies for the one-night showing of the documentary *Eating You Alive*. Need I say more? I woke up the next day a new woman. My conversion to plant-based nutrition was born.

Why a plant-based diet, you might ask? It's a simple answer. After watching the film, doing some reading, and listening to sound advice from friends and family, especially Melissa, it became clear that I should try something that might work to help me feel and get better. It became necessary to correct the bad eating habits I had developed over the years. A drastic change is necessary to prevent or reverse the causes of premature death. I received two presents from Melissa thereafter, back-to-back, both cookbooks, one of which was Dr. Michael Greger's *The How Not to Die Cookbook*. What Greger writes makes sense. "When you decide to eat one food, it means you are choosing not to eat another food . . . there's only so much you can consume in one day. So, whatever you choose has an opportunity cost . . . Every time you put something in your mouth, it's a lost opportunity to invest in something healthier . . . You have about 2,000 calories to spend each day, and each food choice determines whether you are spending them on something that enriches your health or bankrupts it."[1] Something that enriches your health or bankrupts it, how true! Dealing with hypertension, coronary heart disease, or diabetes is bankrupting, wiping out our health. I quickly embraced the seemingly impossible idea of removing meat, salt, sugar, and oil from my diet, for the time being, at the very least. Talk about another discipline routine to add to the mix. I took it one day at a time, three months at a time, under a doctor's care, systematically evaluating its impact on my health. I kept an open mind to the change. Taylor crystallizes the adventure in a few words that I can fully embrace: "Learn to turn to good advantage the unscheduled twist of events which throws your well-laid plans into confusion…The finest self-discipline is seen, not in rigidity, but in resiliency."[2]

Going plant-based became a daily commitment while living with a carnivore. I read package labels when shopping—all the time. Bulk dried beans of assorted colors, brown rice, quinoa, spinach fettuccine, whole grain pasta, fresh vegetables and fruits, the unidentifiable leafy variety from the Asian market, almond/cashew milk, pea milk (yes, but how is that possible), a Mrs. Dash collection, and the blessed Ezekiel low-sodium bread fill the shopping cart. Home cooking became a must. Eli discovered the Instant Pot. Sunday evening routine included the electric pressure-cooking of the bean and grain selections for the week. Thanks to my husband's culinary skills, each homemade dish, although unsalted, was created with attention to herbs, spices, texture, and flavor, whether from the holy trinity of French cooking or the Spanish *sofrito*. Packing my lunch meal became a ritual. However, outside dining tested my resolve. I opted to dine at home unless we visited vegan establishments. I essentially ate seeds and grass. Eli, however, feasted on practically the gamut of the animal kingdom. He likes to put it this way: I am plant-based; he is pork-based. The battle of will was ongoing.

One late afternoon, Eli decided to sauté a homemade hamburger. The grilled aroma did not bother me like it used to. I was typing. The TV was on. I was hardly paying attention to the show when a famous steakhouse commercial distracted me. I looked up. Just as a sizzling steak grazed the screen, I caught a whiff of the hamburger sputtering on the pan. The situation presented a conundrum. I thought, for one second, that the fragrant smell emanating from the kitchen came from the steak off the TV. It was like I had lost my mind. I wanted to give up. I wanted to throw out the strict diet. Why do I have to be so disciplined? I entertained a fleeting thought to quit, but it left just as quickly as it came. One day at a time.

Because of a plant-based diet, my blood pressure readings became normal. I have discovered a new level of energy and strength to increase my exercise routine. I do not have to gulp down an energy drink or need caffeine. The radical change all makes sense, so I do it. I have added fish to my diet since, but I have no problem going vegetarian or vegan occasionally. As I reflect on the experience, without a doubt, I attribute my quick conversion to an unusual way of eating to something I recognize from the past, something I have known all along—the music discipline I practiced all my life. Sterner's words could have been my own. "It was my experience of learning music growing up that had laid the foundation that would help me understand both the mental and spiritual struggles in which I now found myself as I searched for answers."[3] Discipline is familiar. It's been my companion through the years.

Thirdly, I believe what anchors the pursuit of discipline in the different areas of our lives is the pledge to devote ourselves to the spiritual disciplines of prayer, reading, and meditating on the Word of God. It used to be a "hit and miss" attempt. I made several excuses along the way. Being busy doesn't equate to getting down to the nitty-gritty. "Open your mouth and taste, open your eyes and see—how good God is. Blessed are you who run to him [in prayer, in the study of His word]. Worship God if you want the best; worship opens doors to all his goodness."[4] To practice yet another area of discipline, I set up a planned reading and meditating on the Psalms, with prayer time, to accompany my writing journey, music practice, healthy nutrition, and exercise. My prayer has become, "I want to taste and see the goodness of God every day." It is amazing to see how waiting on the Lord manifests in concrete ways every day. You become more aware of His presence and active work in your life. You do not miss the little good things that God throws in your way. You just sit, be still, and watch how God unfolds His plan in your life. It is awe-inspiring.

Surprisingly, on this journey, I had the opportunity to reflect on another aspect of spiritual discipline. My grandfather came from a group of people from the Northern Philippines, the Ilocanos. They are known for their hard-working ethic but also for being not just frugal but stingy. Every penny, in their case, *centavo* counts. I remember Daddy rationing our meals so that we did not overeat. There were never leftovers. We all ate enough, but that was it, just enough. I never remembered eating a lot of snacks or having desserts after a meal. We had desserts occasionally when there was company, but that was about it. The grandchildren might be rewarded a Nestle's Crunch bar for taking home a straight-A report card. Lavish was a bad word—extravagance was forbidden. Daddy's motto was *simple living for simple folks.*

That is what I attribute my stinginess to, which personally translated into not fully trusting God's providence and generosity. I had to learn it the hard way. As an adult, the tithing spirit eventually developed despite my resistance. The Holy Spirit grabbed hold of my heart. God continues to be generous in meeting my needs, restoring broken relationships, and blessing my life. A renewed commitment to give back to the Lord His due portion has been awakened. In this season of my life, the discipline has taken shape into the challenging phase to give above and beyond. During my early research, Johnson University Vice President for External Relations, Dr. Richard Clark, encouraged me to read *The Paradox of Generosity*, a thought-provoking book on tithing and giving. I have been given time to write my story. I do not want to squander the opportunity.

EPILOGUE

I decided to take a trip back to New York City to conduct some research. I was hoping to peruse historical documents and possibly interview folks who might be able to confirm my recollections at both Juilliard and Queens College. I was inspired by Johnson University President Emeritus Dr. Tommy Smith, who had published a book, *Above Every Other Desire*, on the 125-year history of Johnson. I asked him how to go about the research. Tommy gave sound advice on how to sift through archived records. Otherwise, the process may prove quite overwhelming. After contacting the Juilliard Library and Archives through email, I received a response from archivist Jeni Dahmus Farah. She welcomed the idea to pore through historical documents specific to the years I had attended Pre-College and regarding faculty members.

My older daughter, Miriam, accompanied me on this trip. Our daughters were both born in New York: Miriam in upstate New York and Melissa in Long Island. They consider New York their home state. Miriam had just returned from a vacation the month before our trip, a trip that included climbing parts of the Canadian Rockies that span an area from Montana through Alberta. She was in great shape. The morning walks in my Florida neighborhood did not prepare me for the 20,000-steps-a-day regimen of walking the longer blocks of New York City and climbing up and down all the subway stairs—both activities brutally unforgiving to a middle-aged body. Outside of the two appointments at the music schools, we narrowed down the sightseeing list to a few spots. Miriam and I indulged in the visual pleasures at the Museum of Modern Art one afternoon. We sampled the creative concepts of vegan and plant-based nutrition in affluent Tribeca, artsy Chelsea, the fashionable West Village, the trendy Lower East Side, and the sophisticated Rockefeller Center. But towards the end of the week, I just wanted a plain hamburger with lettuce and tomato, well, some kind of bean burger, or better yet, the impossible burger. We met up with cousin Francisco, Uncle and Auntie's son, for an exquisite new dining experience at an award-winning Ayurvedic cuisine establishment. We went through each course. The friendly chef mingled with the customers at each table. We were delighted by its savory and sweet delicacies. We chatted and laughed about how we love our family and also how frustrating they can be sometimes.

Another afternoon, Miriam and I traversed into the belly of Central Park to places I had been forbidden to venture into as a teenager. I finally saw the Bethesda Terrace and Fountain, the Lake, and Strawberry Fields! For more than four decades, I had only walked the perimeter of the park around the green spots closest to the streets. My Uncle and Auntie warned me that Central Park was mostly a dangerous zone in the '70s. But this time, it was Miriam who was the travel guide. What I had missed all those years! I took in every sight, scent, and sound in this peaceful setting. I was so taken by the boats leisurely floating on the lake, their passengers basking under the crisp autumn air. The scene reminded me of Claude Monet's paintings, *Boating on the River* and *The Boat at Giverny*. I casually proposed to Miriam that perhaps we could rent ourselves a boat and that she might consider rowing us around while I take a nap to rest from all the walking. I, unfortunately, did not get my wish.

A month before our trip, we decided we were going to see just one Broadway musical. It was a toss-up between *Frozen* and *Anastasia*. Although I would have loved to have seen my college friend, Debbie Assael-Migliore (our piano trio back in the day included Kathy Livolsi) playing cello in the orchestra part of *Frozen*, *Anastasia* won out. *Anastasia* was an animated musical fantasy film that my daughters loved. So that was an easy choice for me. As usual, the theater was packed. As the show progressed, I began to see the similarity of Anastasia's story of separation from her family to my story. I did not realize that Anastasia's story would resonate more than I cared to admit. When the main character delved into the "Journey to the Past" song, it suddenly dawned on me that our trip followed a parallel path to Anastasia's. Coming back to New York was what Miriam aptly dubbed "Mom's journey to the past" in a later social media post.

But let the main thing be the main thing. The reason for the trip was to visit Juilliard and Queens College to conduct research. First, Juilliard was exactly as I remembered it, except that from the outside, the old main entrance at 66th Street is now the secondary entrance reserved for faculty and students. The Juilliard bookstore constitutes much of that side of the building. The main entrance is now at 65th Street, the same entrance that leads concert-goers to Alice Tully Hall. And yes, both entrances were guarded well. So it helped that we had an appointment. We checked in and got our badges. Thus, began the walk to the hallowed hallways of the revered institution.

We headed straight to the fifth floor where the library is. I quickly glanced at a glass table display of Aaron Copland's score of *El Salón México* by the hallway just outside the library. Yet another turnstile greeted us upon entering the library door. I didn't know that you needed a key card to go through it. I set off the alarm, blaring as I nonchalantly marched through the turnstile. When everyone else calmed down, and our badges assured the folks at the check-out desk that we were legitimate visitors, we waited for archivist Jeni Dahmus Farah.

Faculty and students expeditiously appeared through the turnstile and just as quickly disappeared after finding a particular music score or book, perhaps just before a class. I observed students carrying their distinguishable instrument cases of violin, cello, or clarinet meandering by the hallway outside the glass walls, probably going to or coming out of a lesson on the 5th floor. I wondered which of these young people would become the next Emanuel Ax, Anne-Sophie Mutter, Leonard Bernstein, or Yo-Yo Ma. It was fascinating watching the flow of traffic.

A few folks began to sit at the tables close to where I had parked my belongings. I walked around the room, observing wall portraits and several glass display tables, prominently displaying photographs of printed score pages and historical documents related to distinguished American composer Leonard Bernstein. The Maestro dominated the front landscape of the library.

Ms. Dahmus appeared after a few minutes with an expandable file pocket. She had prepared the documents and photos and meticulously grouped them into file folders for my viewing. After the perfunctory introductions, I immediately observed her passion for her work. She was thorough and extremely detailed as she guided me through the procedures. Finally, after an entire summer of corresponding via email, we found ourselves face-to-face. All at once, we delved into the subjects of the research. We began to talk about people that I had the privilege of knowing but whom she had only read about. She was fascinated with bits of stories I shared with her about my teachers. But I could tell that she did her job well in searching for the historical documents that I might be able to use for my book. I felt like I had known her for a while.

After leading us to a room to check in our bags and water bottles, we returned to the table, ready to work. No water bottle and no pens, only pencils to write with in your notebook, or you could use your laptop—simple instructions to which I gladly obliged. I read and signed a paper to agree to all the rules. I was giddy for a minute, for I was about to go back in time. A hushed moment prefaced what was going to be a few hours of reading. I welcomed the anticipated emotions about to invade my whole being. A good feeling, indeed!

The file on Mr. Munz was astounding. I read the report of the then President of Juilliard, Dr. Peter Mennin, to the Board of Directors in 1963 that included the appointment of Mr. Munz to the piano faculty of Juilliard. His credentials notably highlighted his performances with the New York Philharmonic, the Philadelphia Orchestra, the Boston Symphony, and St. Louis, Cincinnati, and Minneapolis Symphonies, his global concert tours, and his previous teaching posts at the Curtis Institute of Music in Philadelphia and the Peabody Conservatory of Music in Baltimore. An *AMICA* (Automatic Musical Instrument Collectors' Association) magazine in 1977 featured a biographical sketch of Mieczyslaw Munz that included a story that "Professor Munz attended a piano recital by the great Rachmaninoff. After the concert, Munz went backstage to congratulate Rachmaninoff. Rachmaninoff said, 'Get away from here; people keep telling me that you play my rhapsody better than I do.'"[1] This bit of information made me cry. I entertained a whimsical thought that I am only two degrees of separation from Sergei Rachmaninoff! To think of the musical heritage that I have! I was beyond astounded. I happen to possess a downloaded 1941 recording of Mr. Munz's performance of the *Rachmaninoff Rhapsody on a Theme by Paganini* (the pianofiles.com) with the National Orchestral Association, conducted by Leon Barzin. It is believed that it may have been Munz's final public performance. Mr. Munz was brilliant, and yes, he played very fast.

Coincidentally, Mr. Leon Pommers taught me the same Rachmaninoff *Rhapsody*. I won a young artists' concerto competition with that concerto and performed it with the orchestra. The Rachmaninoff connections were becoming more pronounced as I continued to research Mr. Munz. Romantic music, in general, seemed to beckon me to embrace its composers without hesitation. Chopin is probably my favorite Romantic composer if I had to choose just one. I have always gravitated to Chopin's music. Rachmaninoff was not even on my radar for a long time. I didn't even study any of his *Preludes*. So it's interesting to note that way back in the Philippines, Mrs. Brimo selected for me to learn the Rachmaninoff *Concerto #3 in D Minor* shortly after I had performed the *Gershwin Rhapsody in Blue* several times. I played the first movement of the Rachmaninoff piece for the master class of Mr. Munz the summer before I left Manila for New York. Reading the article at the Juilliard Library and Archives connected all the dots for me.

Several photos of Munz's younger years of performing and teaching emerged from the files. One photo captured his dashing looks for the promotion of his second Aeolian Hall recital in 1922 and his 1926 Carnegie Hall recital. There were other formal and informal photos of Munz, including one of him and the Juilliard piano faculty from 1971 in celebration of a colleague. His tall stature made him stand above the rest of the faculty. I sat in awe as I carefully held the historical gems, but more importantly, in humble appreciation of the legacy Munz left behind. He was truly a high-caliber pedagogue! I was most captivated by one picture of Munz standing in his studio giving a lesson. It was how I remembered him.

The next file folders held the documents of the Pre-College Division. I examined the catalogs specific to the early years I attended, which listed the names of my theory, keyboard studies, and solfège teachers, as well as the detailed requirements for auditions. I had also requested Ms. Dahmus pull out files on my theory and keyboard studies teacher, Ms. Frances Goldstein. Ms. Goldstein was a rock-star teacher. According to the school catalog, Frances Goldstein was born in New York. She graduated from The Juilliard School, formerly named the Institute of Musical Arts. She also attended Pius X School of Liturgical Music and studied piano with Zofia Naimska. She taught at Juilliard since 1930. Ms. Goldstein left an indelible mark on my musical development. Her approach to theory keyboard studies was unmatched. She was a no-nonsense, tough teacher. An engaging piece of information emerged from the records. An article from a trade magazine *Record World* in 1976 by Fredric Gershon revealed an anecdotal reminiscence of his good friend and legendary American pop singer, composer, pianist, and producer, Neil Sedaka. Ms. Goldstein was one of Gershon and Sedaka's teachers at Juilliard. Gershon revealed that Sedaka was a phenomenal pianist who was loved by the teachers; however, Sedaka suffered the high-brow attitude and tension between himself and the classical pianists, especially when Sedaka crossed over to pop music and began writing songs for actress Connie Francis. Gershon also quickly noted that American composer and Emmy, Grammy, Oscar, and Tony awardee Marvin Hamlisch also studied under Ms. Goldstein. It's common knowledge that Hamlisch was probably one of the most famous alumni of Queens College. But to have read that Hamlisch was also a by-product of Frances Goldstein's superb pedagogy at Juilliard was all too much information to process in one day.

Ms. Dahmus also escorted us to the teaching studios on the same fifth floor. The solemn walk on the familiar hallowed hallways flooded my mind with happy and good memories. While Miriam was snapping away photos on her smartphone, I kept thinking to myself, *Yes, Ruth, you've walked these steps before!* Ms. Dahmus asked me if anything looked familiar. I pointed to the door at the end of the hallway. "This is the hallway that led to Mr. Munz's studio. I think Ms. DeLay might have taught in that corner room." Dorothy DeLay-Wieniawski was a distinguished violin teacher whose students included Itzhak Perlman, Midori, and Sarah Chang. Ms. Dahmus delightedly confirmed that the door, indeed, opens to the late Ms. DeLay's teaching studio and that it is now the studio of Professor Itzhak Perlman. Ms. Dahmus then explained that renovations over the years required that several rooms be reconfigured, one of which was Mr. Munz's studio, which used to be next to Ms. DeLay's.

We walked back to the library to discuss the next steps of securing permission for publication and other protocols to follow. We said our goodbyes. I thoroughly appreciated

Jeni's detailed work and her gracious cooperation and assistance. Miriam and I quickly made our way down to the second floor to check out the new Pre-College offices. Then I wanted to march straight to the practice rooms on the fourth floor, and so we did! We walked around, with each corner leading us to endless hallways of practice rooms. After passing through practice rooms where string and woodwind players hang out, we finally reached the area where all the music that rang through the corridors were the familiar passages of the great piano works of the great masters. We made it to the piano practice row. The passages resounded through the doors, some Chopin, some Ravel, some Liszt, some Beethoven, some Scriabin, as though these composers appeared to be engrossed in a random musical conversation. I found joy in trying to name each tune. I scurried from room to room, peering through the little window to catch a glimpse of the young artist so riveted by the pages and pages of music. I thought of each student's goal of logging in the hours of practice. It's a life of discipline that these students have chosen, one that will bring a lifetime of rewards, a lesson well learned by this musician. It was a good visit, after all.

The following day presented a new agenda: Navigate the train and bus to reach the Aaron Copland School of Music at Queens College (QC) in the borough of Queens. The last time I was on campus was 1988, the last year I taught at the Copland Preparatory Studies Division. Since then, QC has become the home of the arts in Queens. I wanted to take Miriam on the same train and city bus I used to ride on my way to QC. Upon reaching the street from the subway to catch the bus, I got disoriented for a moment as the bus stop was no longer at the street corner I remembered. The once single-roofed shopping mall (yes, the same mall where the hold-up robbery occurred decades before) has now quadrupled into several blocks. We eventually found the bus stop on the other side of one of the buildings.

The bus route took us through my once familiar neighborhood, the corner where I hailed the garbage collector. For a second there, I felt like I was nineteen again. My mind briefly wandered to the past. I pictured myself sitting in the back of the bus, in my plaid winter coat with a fleece collar, studying for an exam while a group of rowdy high school parochial students got on the next stop. I remember it was always an interestingly noisy ride at rush hour. In about 20 minutes, the bus dropped us off just a few yards from the side entrance steps that led to the 2,124-seat Colden Auditorium. I began videotaping the stroll down memory lane. I whispered, "I played the Rachmaninoff *Rhapsody* in that building!" Around the bend from Colden on the left is Rathaus Hall, which formerly housed the Music Department and is now home to the Department of Drama, Theatre, and Dance. Just a few steps across Rathaus is the newer building of the Aaron Copland School of Music (ACSM). The building holds three auditoriums: the LeFrak Concert Hall, a beautiful 489-seat room and the Choral Room, which seats 165, and the Recital Room for smaller audiences under 100.

I had arranged to meet with Dr. Edward Smaldone for

an interview. Smaldone and I were music majors back in the day. He hired me to teach at the Center for Preparatory Studies in Music at QC while I was pursuing graduate work. Dr. Smaldone received the "Composer of the Year" award in 2016 from the Classical Recording Foundation. His music has been performed in the United States, Japan, China, Germany, and the Czech Republic, to name a few. He was Director of the ACSM for 14 years, and at the time of the visit, was back to teaching music theory and composition and was the Associate Director of ACSM. He gave us a quick tour of the magnificent building with natural light emanating from the atrium onto the second-floor classrooms that wrap around the building.

I briefly ran into Dr. Joel Mandelbaum, a professor emeritus and former Chair of the Music Department in the 1970s. Surprisingly he remembered me, my maiden name that is. Dr. Mandelbaum, a composer, whose PhD dissertation was the first on microtonality composition. His trademark scholarly and artistic demeanor relished the fact that QC still invites him to teach one course a semester of his choosing. It just so happened that at the time of this writing, Mandelbaum was teaching Theory IV. I seized the opportunity to brag about my own Theory IV students, past and present. The remaining concepts of their class required exploring bitonality, non-functional tonality, and twelve-tone technique, in addition to extended and chromatic harmony. I told Mandelbaum that these students knew it was not a walk in the park, yet they stayed disciplined, persevered, and finished well. Dr. Joel Mandelbaum also expounded on the intentional architectural design of not installing windows on the outside of the building, primarily to eliminate the noise of the Long Island Expressway that sits just a block away from the building, and instead position the classroom windows on the inside walls, open into the atrium with its natural lighting. Brilliant idea! Then I noticed the scores and notebooks Mandelbaum was carrying. He said he's still composing. I asked if I could take a peek at his new compositions, still notated in pencil. That was a highlight of the day for me.

I've been reflecting on the multidimensional academic climate that I encountered at QC. Leon Pommers was the professor who, in my opinion, made the greatest impact on my life during my undergraduate and graduate years of study. Thoughts of QC elicited warm and happy memories. I thought about what made QC and ACSM stand out. I knew that something extraordinary happened in that place, but I wanted to understand more. I finally began to take inventory of the significance of QC after reading a doctoral dissertation by Peter Archer on the *History of the Queens College Music Department.*

The Bachelor of Music degree at QC was a four-and-a-half year degree. The rigor of performance training was comparable to my previous conservatory training: lessons in your primary instrument, chamber music work, and large ensembles such as orchestra and choir. Performance majors were required to play at a recital of some sort each semester; performance at a chamber music recital with your assigned group was also required, as well as participating in the choir or orchestra concerts. In addition, performance majors studied theory, sight singing and ear training, music history, analysis, conducting, orchestration, and composition classes with distinguished faculty in their respective fields. I always wondered why the curriculum was demanding for a city college or a small music program in a liberal arts college. I did not complain. I was enjoying studying music again. The history of the department included the long, deliberate process of becoming the Aaron Copland School of Music that began in 1980. It explained the reason for the rigor of the curriculum. There was already a plan in place to move towards a conservatory-like curriculum even before I became a QC student. It looked like we were the beneficiaries of a strategic plan to become the kind of institution that would be the musical center in Queens, competitive among other regarded schools, and endorsed by and bearing the name of the great American composer of the 20th century, Aaron Copland.

I sat down with Smaldone to reminisce on the richness of our shared heritage. He articulated the high points of history. "[Karol] Rathaus and other people that were early faculty of the college were just outstanding people, and they hired more people like them. By the time we got into the 1970s when we were in school, we had a faculty that had Barry Brook, Carl Schachter, Charles Burkhart, George Perle, Hugo Weisgall, Henry Weinberg, Leo Kraft, Howard Brofsky, Raymond Erickson, Joseph Machlis, John Castellini, Joel Mandelbaum . . . In a department of 25, when you have nine or ten people with a real international impact on the level of Carl Schachter,

Charles Burkhart, George Perle, it's kind of astounding for a little city university."[2] I agree. Somehow, I knew back then that there was something special about the place. I might have taken it for granted, but truth be told, I was fortunate to have experienced the invigorating and unique learning environment under composers and theorists who converged at one location at a particular time period, not at the more prestigious borough of Manhattan, but rather in Queens. I studied under six of the twelve aforementioned, whether it's counterpoint or Schenkerian analysis (Schachter), advanced analysis (Kraft), composition (Weinberg), or performance practice of a musical period (Erickson); one professor was my master's thesis advisor (Brofsky), two were chamber music coaches (Weisgall and Erickson). It never ceased to amaze me the high caliber of the QC music faculty. As I previously wrote, these folks are in the music dictionary. Smaldone further explained, "In addition, over the course of the late '50s and '60s, people like Luigi Dallapiccola and Elliott Carter [were] here. These were the kinds of people that, because of the reputation of the other faculty, said yes, that should look like a good idea . . . we were not a terribly good fit, at that time, for Dallapiccola and Carter, but they were here."[3] I was so thrilled to hear about our student days within a historical context.

The QC visit turned out to be more enlightening than I had expected. It gave me pause to be thankful again for what I have been privileged to experience. Here is my best effort to explain this period in my life. It was the closest thing to living as though I had been transported back into the 19th century. The decades of the '70s and the '80s at QC evoked a time of intellectual and artistic synergy, an environment much like the Romantic period. For such a time, a group of gifted modern composers graced our presence, walked the hallways with the students, chatted with us, ate with us in the cafeteria, attended our concerts, taught us our craft, and assessed our progress with honesty and kindness. Collegiality was at its best. What an honor to have sat at the feet of men and women who deeply cared about their students! I learned the lesson while a student at the Aaron Copland School of Music and filed it away: *It's possible to have a group of talented, eccentric musicians in one building at the same time. How fortunate we (the students) were to have been mentored by a nurturing faculty who fostered a healthy environment of competition, and modeled an appreciation and respect for one another.* This lesson inspired me. It's possible to recreate the same environment if and when given a chance to do so in another academic institution. I truly believe that I am the way I am, and I teach the way I do, because of the encouraging and dynamic educators who showed me the way. The importance of a solid education is something I never need any convincing to advocate. Perhaps all that I have experienced is why I decided to become a teacher.

Paterson ends his book *The Life That You Were Meant to Live* with a LifePlan he developed to facilitate a life journey for anyone who might follow a roadmap for his or her life. It takes discipline and commitment to walk through the prescriptive plan to discover and flesh out your unique purpose in life. The LifePlan is one way to take the journey of discovering God's purpose in your life. Life is a journey, but it is about how to take it to the end with purpose and meaning. I describe myself on social media as a teacher, wife, and mama trying to finish well—to finish the sojourn that is called life.

The Book of Joshua in the Bible is a call to leadership, a sojourn to take his nation to cross the Jordan to reach the land promised to Israel since the days of Abraham. The story of Ruth unfolds the challenges of her journey with her mother-in-law, Naomi, but also details her tenacity towards reaching redemption. The psalmist describes life as traversing through lush meadows, quiet waters, and valleys of the shadow of death to dwell in the Lord's house forever. The apostle Paul calls it a race. Finish the race; take it to the end; end well. Jesus calls Himself the Way, the Truth, the Life—that He is the road to His Father's house, the house with many rooms He is preparing for us, the culmination of the journey of a Christ follower. Each of us takes a similar journey that eventually will end or culminate at a specific juncture. A good dose of discipline and the practice of good habits surely will help along the way. They provide the scaffolding to assist us in completing the journey to end well.

The kind of discipline I propose in this book consists of the direction and the good habits established at a young age. They have been framed by the unique experiences of growing up as a child prodigy. But what if a person has not been given the opportunity for self-discovery early in life? What if, due to extenuating circumstances, the search for purpose and meaning comes at a much later time? Is it, then, too late to pursue an intentional plan? Mark Montemayor, a longtime friend, former business executive, and pastor, weighs in on the matter. Working as a leadership consultant and life coach now, he fully understands the importance of being intentional about life and leadership. I asked him: "What does 'it's never too late to start' mean?" Montemayor offered a thoughtful response: "Regardless of how much of your journey is behind you or how much is still ahead of you, systematically identifying your specific talents, your life calling, and mapping out a specific plan gives you the best chance to fully realize your God-given potential. Regardless of whether you have two years or two decades to work with, making the most of the opportunities God gives you is always a good choice. Tom [Paterson] loved to ask: 'What kind of return is God getting on the investment He's made in you?' Understanding how to do that—regardless of the method you use to figure that out—helps maximize that return for God."[4] I couldn't agree more.

Life is a journey, but it is about how to take it to the end with purpose and meaning.

From Manila to Juilliard to Queens College, building a private teaching studio, freelancing, a stint with Yamaha Music Education System, worship ministries at Port Jefferson, New York, and Princeton Community Church, New Jersey, teaching at Seminole State College and Florida Christian College, then Johnson University, to being a pianist at Walt Disney Entertainment, and retirement; every step of the way leads to a final destination. A better book title could have been *From Juilliard to JU to the House of a Famous Mouse.* This has been my journey. I'm not there yet, but it's coming. The horizon draws near. The privilege is mine to tell my story integrated into lessons on discipline and good habits. I have been surrounded by a caring family, an exceptional roster of teachers, a string of blessed opportunities, and a steadfast faith, all guiding me from my younger years into my adult life. If this is the life I was meant to live, I fully embrace it, with its ups and downs, warts and all, through periods of joy and accomplishment, loneliness, and failures. Each season of life brings new challenges. When a crisis gets resolved, another one springs up. Life is hard as it is, and nothing is certain in this world because of its fallen nature. However, life is harder without a purpose. The struggle continues to the very end. When you think about what else could go wrong, something does. God reigns just the same. Going back home to Him, from whom all things came to be, is the ultimate goal. God is our final destination. He is the Beginning and the End. And so we endure until then. I am a former child prodigy, a teacher, a wife, and a mama, loved beyond measure, covered by God's incomparable grace, continuing the sojourn in the meantime, trying to end well, no matter what.

The psalmist describes life as traversing through lush meadows, quiet waters, and valleys of the shadow of death to dwell in the Lord's house forever.

NOTES

Chapter 1

1. Discipline. (n.d.). In *Oxford English Dictionary* online. https://www.oxfordlearnersdictionaries.com/us/definition/english/discipline_1?q=discipline.
2. Ibid.
3. Gordon, S. (2006). *Mastering the art of performance.* Oxford University Press, p. 67.
4. Buscaglia, L. F. (1982). *Living, loving and learning.* New York: Fawcett Columbine.
5. Paterson, T. (1998). *The life you were meant to live.* Nashville, TN: Thomas Nelson Publishers. p. 75.
6. Fink, S. (1992). *Mastering piano technique: A guide for students, teachers, and performers.* Portland, OR: Amadeus Press, p.13.
7. Holy Bible, *New International Version*, Matthew 26:41.
8. Ibid, Luke 16:10.

Chapter 2

1. Sterner, T. M. (2012). *The practicing mind: Developing focus and discipline in your life.* Novato, CA: New World Library, p. xiv.
2. Ibid, 65.
3. Smith. C., & Davidson, H. (2014.) *The paradox of generosity: Giving we receive, grasping we lose.* Oxford University Press, p.13.

4. Paterson, p. 168.

5. Holy Bible, *New International Version*, 2 Corinthians 9:6.

6. Paterson, pp. 13-14.

7. Klickstein, G. (2009). *The musician's way: Guide to practice, performance, and wellness.* Oxford University Press, p. 3.

8. QuoteFancy. (n.d.). *Ignacy Jan Paderewski quotes.* https://quotefancy.com/ignacy-jan-paderewski-quotes.

9. Sterner, p. 65.

10. Ibid, p. 66.

11. Stephen Curry (Interviewee), & ASAP Sports (Interviewer). (2015, May 4). *Golden State Warriors media conference* [Interview transcript]. Retrieved from http://www.asapsports.com/show_conference. php?id=108794

12. Jeffreys, I., & Moody, J. (Eds.). (2016). *Strength and conditioning for sports performance.* Routledge, p. 373.

13. Taylor, R. S. (1962). *The Disciplined Life.* Minneapolis: Bethany House, p. 98.

14. Whipple, T., & Eckhardt, R. B. (2011). *The Endurance Paradox.* Walnut Creek, CA: Left Coast Press, p. 157.

15. Sterner, p. xvi.

Chapter 3

1. Taylor, p. 106.

2. Gordon, p. 68.

3. Ibid, p. 67.

4. Ibid, p. 69.

5. Schiller, J. F. V. (2010, August 19). *Quote by Schiller, Johann Friedrich Von on patience.* Quotations Book.

6. Paterson, p. 11.

7. Miller, J. (2023, July). *Parables; The talents* [Video]. YouTube, https://youtu.be/PxoZEzesiSI?feature=shared

8. Paterson, p. 14.

Chapter 6

1. www.juilliard.edu.

Chapter 7

1. Overdorf, D. *Finishing the sojourn well.* Knoxville: Johnson University. CD, 11-07-2013 JU.

2. Krzywicki, P. (2016). *From Paderewski to Penderecki.* Lulu Publishing Services, p. 43.

3. Ibid, p. 44.

4. Ibid, p. 44.

5. Walker, A. (2005). *Reflections of Liszt.* Ithaca: Cornell University Press, p. 207.

6. Paterson, p. 75.

7. Ibid, p. 168.

8. Aniela Rubinstein, 93; widow of famed pianist. (2002, January 6). Los Angeles Times. https://www.latimes.com/archives/la-xpm-2002-jan-06-me-20697-story.html.

9. Ax, E. (2018, September 24). Phone interview with Emanuel Ax.

10. Sterner, pp. 97-98.

11. Ax interview.

12. Whipple & Eckhardt, p. 159.
13. Ax interview.
14. Ibid.
15. Krzywicki, pp. 125-126.
16. Ibid, p. 125.
17. Ibid, p. 128.
18. Bellman, J. D., & Goldberg, H. (Eds.). (2017). *Chopin and his world.* Princeton University Press, p. 288.
19. Ibid, p. 290.
20. Gordon, p. 110.
21. Ibid, p. 111.
22. Krzywicki, p. 125.
23. Lester, J. (2001, June 8). *Paid notice: Death of Leon Pommers. The New York Times*, Section C.
24. Smaldone, E. (2014, May 7). Leo Kraft (1922-2014). New Music Box. New Music USA. Retrieved December 10, 2018 from https://nmbx.newmusicusa.org.
25. Ibid.

Chapter 11

1. Sterner, p. 96.
2. Hardin, L., & Hartley, G. (Eds.). (2012). *Rooted in Christ.* Florida Christian College, pp. 53-55.
3. Da Vinci quotes. (n.d.). Goodreads. Retrieved December 2, 2024, from https://www.goodreads.com/quotes/tag/da-vinci.
4. Ovid quotes. (n.d.). Goodreads. Retrieved December 2, 2024, from https://www.goodreads.com/quotes/tag/ovid.

Chapter 12

1. Greger, M. (2017) *The how not to die cookbook.* New York: Flatiron Books, p. 194.
2. Taylor, p. 106.
3. Sterner, p. 3.
4. Holy Bible, *The Message*, Psalms 34:8-9.

Epilogue

1. *AMICA Bulletin*, Biographical sketches. *AMICA Bulletin*, 14 (3), 73.
2. Smaldone, E. (2018, October 19). Personal Interview with Dr. Edward Smaldone. Flushing, New York.
3. Ibid.
4. Montemayor, M. (2024, December 2). Personal communication with Mark Montemayor.

BIBLIOGRAPHY

AMICA Bulletin. (1977). Biographical sketches. *AMICA Bulletin*, 14 (3), 73.

Aniela Rubinstein, 93; widow of famed pianist. (2002, January 6). *Los Angeles Times.* https://www.latimes.com/ archives/la-xpm-2002-jan-06-me-20697-story.html.

Ax, E. (2018, September 24). Phone interview with Emanuel Ax.

Bellman, J. D., & Goldberg, H. (Eds.). (2017). *Chopin and his world*. Princeton University Press.

Buscaglia, L. F. (1982). *Living, loving and learning.* New York: Fawcett Columbine.

Curry, S. (Interviewee), & ASAP Sports (Interviewer). (2015, May 4). *Golden State Warriors media conference* [Interview transcript]. Retrieved from http://www.asapsports.com/ show_conference.php?id=108794.

Da Vinci quotes. (n.d.). Goodreads. Retrieved December 2, 2024, from https://www.goodreads.com/quotes/tag/ da-vinci.

Discipline. (n.d.). In Oxford English Dictionary online. Retrieved from https://www.oxfordlearnersdictionaries.com/ us/definition/english/discipline_1?q=discipline.

Fink, S. (1992). *Mastering piano technique: A guide for students, teachers, and performers.* Portland: Amadeus Press.

Gordon, S. (2006). *Mastering the art of performance.* Oxford University Press, 2006.

Greger, M. (2017). *The how not to die cookbook*. New York: Flatiron Books.

Hardin, L., & Hartley, G. (Eds.). (2012). *Rooted in Christ*. Florida Christian College.

Holy Bible, *The Message*.

Holy Bible, *New International Version*.

Jeffreys, I., & Moody, J. (Eds.). (2016). *Strength and conditioning for sports performance*. Routledge.

Klickstein, G. (2009). *The musician's way: Guide to practice, performance, and wellness*. Oxford University Press.

Krzywicki, P. (2016). *From Paderewski to Penderecki*. Lulu Publishing Services.

Lester, J. (2001, June 8). *Paid notice: Death of Leon Pommers*. *The New York Times*.

Miller, J. (2023, July). *Parables; The talents* [Video]. YouTube https://youtu.be/PxoZEzesiSI?feature=shared.

Montemayor, M. (2024, December 2). Personal communication with Mark Montemayor.

Overdorf, D. (2013, November 7). *Finishing the sojourn well*. [CD] Knoxville: Johnson University.

Ovid quotes. (n.d.). Goodreads. Retrieved December 2, 2024, from https://www.goodreads.com/quotes/tag/ovid.

Oxford University Press. (n.d.). Discipline. In Oxford English Dictionary online. https://www.oxfordlearnersdictionaries.com/us/definition/english/discipline_1?q=discipline.

Paterson, T. (1998). *The life you were meant to live*. Nashville: Thomas Nelson Publishers.

QuoteFancy. (n.d.). Ignacy Jan Paderewski quotes. QuoteFancy. https://www.quotefancy.com/ignacy-jan-paderewski-quotes

Schiller, J. F. V. (2010, August 19). Quote by Schiller, Johann Friedrich Von on Patience. *Quotations Book.*

Smaldone, E. (2018, October 19). Personal Interview with Dr. Edward Smaldone. Flushing, New York.

Smaldone, E. (2014, May 7). Leo Kraft (1922-2014): Spiky, tart, and fierce but also sweet and gentle. New Music Box. New Music USA. https://nmbx.newmusicusa.org.

Smith. C., & Davidson, H. (2014). *The paradox of generosity: Giving we receive, grasping we lose.* Oxford University Press.

Sterner, T. M. (2012). *The practicing mind: Developing focus and discipline in your life.* Novato, CA: New World Library.

Taylor, R. S. (1962). *The disciplined life.* Minneapolis: Bethany House.

Walker, A. (2005). *Reflections of Liszt.* Ithaca, NY: Cornell University Press.

Whipple, T., & Eckhardt, R. B. (2011). *The Endurance Paradox.* Walnut Creek, CA: Left Coast Press.

www.juilliard.edu

ACKNOWLEDGMENTS

I am deeply grateful to my family, the Acoba, Topacio, and Reyes families. You are the solid anchor of the book. My story is intricately woven into the bigger story of our heritage rooted in our motherland country and tested in our collective journey to the other side of the world. You are all my inspiration.

To my friends and colleagues who walked alongside me, your support has been unmatched. I'm extremely grateful to Arron Chambers. You encouraged me to write my story, and you singlehandedly pushed me to accomplish my dream through years of trepidation and insecurities. Thanks to Marla Black, my trustworthy librarian colleague, for editing the endnotes and bibliography list. Special thanks to Twila Sias and Marla Black for being my dedicated proofreaders. I'm deeply indebted to Johnson University, Dr. Matthew Broaddus, and Dr. Jon Weatherly for sending me off on a sabbatical to jumpstart the writing project.

I cannot begin to express my gratitude to Mr. Emanuel Ax and Dr. Edward Smaldone whose thoughtful and insightful interviews paid tribute to teachers, professors, and mentors who modeled excellence, tenacity, and devotion to their craft and whose brilliant minds we hold in the highest esteem. I sincerely thank Jeni Dahmus Farah for providing the gems of historical and anecdotal documents from the Juilliard Archives and walking with me down memory lane and the hallways.

I sincerely thank my production and editorial team: Carol Goodlet, Jessica Conley, Adrian Traurig, Nicole Tillotson, Sarah Williams, Sarah Tavoularis, and Claudia Volkman. I am beyond thrilled to have chosen Two Penny Publishing. Tom and Carol Goodlet, you contacted me at the right time. Your friendship knows no bounds.

I appreciate Steffany Morel's much-needed extra encouragement to get my book published. To my trusted nook table and bench, thank you once again for enduring more scuffed markings. You remain my favorite writing spot.

Finally, to all my former students, I appreciate you lending me your ears in the studio, classroom, on tour, and stage. Bloom where you are planted and make a difference in someone's life. Chalis Stefani, Stephanie Gonter, Chad Harris, Morgan Bender, Janna Bartoli, Matt Boden, Joyce Boden, John Howard, Jessica Lup, Kayla Bowman, Karissa Mead, Catheryn Van Kley, Jordan Mishoe, Emily Godwin, Windy Cobourne, Micah Hardin, Audrey Olsheske, Harold Rodriguez, Laurie Brooks, Victoria Wold Lane, Debbie Mejia, Ron Sieber, Joshua McGrew, Tyler Lemmel, Tammy White, Cindy Smith, Beth Sterner, Christina Montgomery Bottley, William Daniels, Laura Kim Ngai, keep the music going. No matter what, take it to the end.

Soli Deo Gloria!

ABOUT THE AUTHOR

 **Ruth Topacio Reyes, Ed.D.**, originally from Manila, Philippines, is a retired professor of music and assistant dean of the School of Communication and Creative Arts of Johnson University. She taught piano, music theory, music history, music appreciation, and practical worship leadership courses. She studied at the Juilliard School Pre-College Division. She received a Bachelor of Music and a Master of Arts in piano performance from Queens College, New York, and a Doctorate in Higher Education Leadership from Nova Southeastern University.

Ruth has performed as a recital soloist, chamber musician, orchestral soloist, and art song and choral accompanist. She has also served in worship ministries in Long Island, New York, Princeton, New Jersey, and Tampa, Florida. She is a pianist for Walt Disney Entertainment, an accompanist for Heart for the Arts Central Florida, and a partner recruitment manager for Two Penny Publishing. Ruth is married with two grown daughters.

But as for me, the nearness of God is my good. I have made the Lord God my refuge, that I may tell of all Thy works.

PSALM 73:28 (NASB)